A ROOM BY ROOM GUIDE

JAPANESE STYLE at HOME

First published in the United Kingdom in 2019 by
Thames & Hudson Ltd, 181A High Holborn, London WC1V 7QX

© 2019 Quarto Publishing plc

This book was designed and produced by
The Bright Press, an imprint of the Quarto Group
The Old Brewery
6 Blundell Street
London N7 9BH

British Library Cataloguing-in-Publication Data
A catalogue record for this book is available from the British Library

ISBN 978-0-500-29499-4

Printed and bound in China

To find out about all our publications, please visit **www.thamesandhudson.com**.
There you can subscribe to our e-newsletter, browse or download our current
catalogue, and buy any titles that are in print.

A ROOM BY ROOM GUIDE

JAPANESE STYLE at HOME

Olivia Bays, Tony Seddon
and Cathelijne Nuijsink

Thames & Hudson

Contents

Preface

There is something irresistible about Japanese-style interiors. It's not always easy to define exactly what constitutes Japanese design, but the emotions inspired by Japanese homes are consistent. They are calming, tranquil spaces; homes where much thought and consideration goes into every element. They may be traditional or modern, made of natural materials or synthetically constructed, playful or serious, but they always invite reflection and contemplation, offering sanctuary from a busy world.

Evolving out of the country's long-standing Shinto and Buddhist roots, Japanese style is grounded in simple principles. Harmony with nature is incredibly important: buildings are designed around external views and are built in ways that coexist with the wider environment around them. Simplicity is key: Zen Buddhist philosophy values spartan, empty spaces, and this translates directly into homes and gardens. Japanese-style interiors are beautiful, but their beauty derives from understated sources: an appreciation of ageing and change, of the fleeting nature of life, of clean lines, contrasting textures and subtle details. Nothing shouts for your attention, but if you look closely, you will be richly rewarded.

Creating your own Japanese-style home is not just about buying the right pieces or faithfully sticking to a rigid set of rules. It's about mood and feelings, about the ways in which you experience your environment. How you arrange each room, and how objects within them relate to each other, is just as important as what each item looks like.

This book will show you how Japanese design as we know it today has evolved, drawing on its traditions but never being hobbled by them. The great achievement of contemporary Japanese design is to use the past as a source of inspiration from which to experiment and innovate, to fuse old and new, East and West, to create new forms that feel fresh yet still quintessentially Japanese. It will show you how to incorporate Japanese style into your own home, how to translate and apply the principles behind Japanese design to each room to create spaces that feel inviting, relaxing and personal to you.

▶ *Sliding screens are classically Japanese and give your home flexibility, allowing you to open up and close off spaces for different occasions.*

1. INTRODUCING
JAPANESE STYLE

Understanding Japanese style

To understand Japanese style, you could do a lot worse than starting with one word: Zen. Brought from China to Japan in the 12th century, Zen Buddhism's guiding principles extend to all aspects of Japanese life, including design. Zen philosophy sets out seven elements for achieving *wabi-sabi*, the distinctly Japanese art of embracing the imperfect and the impermanent. They include: asymmetry or irregularity (*fukinsei*); simplicity (*kanso*); naturalness without pretence (*shizen*); and a focus only on the essential (*koko*).

The roots of Japanese minimalism can be traced back to the mantra of Zen, 'vast emptiness, nothing holy'. The result is a mindful approach to design, involving disciplined editing and an awareness of the importance of space. Interiors are deliberately simple yet enriched by detail; craftsmanship is honoured but natural materials are emphasized over design. Japanese design epitomizes Mies van der Rohe's famous dictum, 'Less is more' – or, as architecture professor Michael Mönninger puts it, 'more with less'.

Traditionally, Japanese houses tend to have a flexibility to them, to feel somehow light. Their floor plans are open and flowing, merging indoor and outdoor spaces. They contain minimal furniture and decoration and can be used for different things at different times. This evolved partly as a practical

response to Japan's geographical and historical context: as a country prone to earthquakes and with limited space and a large population, the Japanese have long been used to living agilely and compactly. It can also be seen as arising from Japan's Buddhist roots and the sense that life is transient and fleeting.

Although shaped by tradition, Japanese design is by no means wedded to it. Designers such as Oki Sato, Shiro Kuramata and Naoto Fukasawa have each found new ways to hold on to the spirit of their country's traditions while innovating for the future. Skilled manufacturers like Tendo Mokko and Maruni Wood Industry have been able to fuse classic craftsmanship with elements of mass production to create high-quality furniture that feels as good as it looks, while Muji has pioneered its highly successful brand of simple utilitarian products and furniture around the world.

Contemporary Japanese interiors often display a balance between, or attempt to reconcile, the contrasting elements of the Japanese character: traditional and modern, East and West, playful and serious, loud and quiet. What unifies them above all else is an appreciation of and connection to nature, to the rhythm of the seasons and the passing of time.

◄ *A kimono hung on the wall makes for an unusual and unique piece of artwork.*

►▲ *A modern take on traditional Japanese style, with untreated wood panels instead of the bamboo screens typically used.*

► *The muted colours and flowing organic shapes of these vases make for a calming display.*

What is Japanese style?

Originally derived from Chinese and other Asian nations, it wasn't until the Asuka period (538–710) and the arrival of Buddhism that a Japanese architectural style began to take shape. Buddhist temples in Japan initially copied Chinese layouts, with spacious courtyards and symmetrical features. Over time they evolved to reflect local tastes, with asymmetrical designs and gardens becoming more popular.

In the following period, the Heian (794–1185), Japanese architecture developed further, using partitions to divide spaces. Pine, cypress and larch were used to make wooden sliding walls and floors. The Kamakura and Muromachi periods (1185–1333 and 1336–1573 respectively) saw

the birth of the teahouse, which in turn had an effect on residential design. In the 16th century, Japanese design began to be set down in codes: detailed outdoor gardens, exterior verandas, decorative *fusuma* (sliding panels) and *byōbu* (folding screens), and the use of *tokonoma* (a built-in recess space) to display art or flowers.

There is a spiritual element to traditional Japanese design. Sen no Rikyū, the 16th-century Japanese tea master, believed that tea should be worshipped for its divine and natural properties. His influence led to teahouses being built with natural materials: bamboo, wood and paper. *Sukiya-zukuri* architecture incorporated teahouse aesthetics, shunning opulence in favour of a refined, understated style, and also affected residential design. It was the start of Japanese minimalism, not only in terms of the way a building looked, but also how it was inhabited.

East meets West

Tokyo was formed during the Edo period, which stretched from 1603 to 1868. Its population grew and the resulting constraints on space led to residential townhouses becoming two-storey. Most Japanese people, however, were farmers until the early 20th century: *minka* (farmhouses) varied in design but were generally wooden with thatched roofs. Kitchens had earth floors, with raised wooden floors for other living spaces.

◄ *Sōri Yanagi's iconic 1954 Butterfly Stool has never been out of production: its graceful curves have been likened to the gates of a Shinto shrine.*

From the late 19th century onwards, Western influences started to penetrate Japan. Architects such as Frank Lloyd Wright and Le Corbusier were invited to the country to teach building design. The influencing was mutual; traditional Japanese design had a big impact on European and American sensibilities. The arts and crafts movement copied the refined, understated quality of Japanese art, while designers such as Charles Rennie Mackintosh and Eileen Gray studied lacquer techniques to meet a demand for Japanese-style furniture.

Following his travels in Japan, Wright based much of his thinking about modern architecture on Japanese-inspired principles. In turn, those principles became tenets of the architectural Modern Movement and the International Style architects of the 1920s and 1930s.

A nation reborn

In the years following the Second World War, Japan transformed from a country damaged by conflict into a powerful manufacturer, leading the way in many industries. The 1950s witnessed the creation of a number of Japanese design institutions, such as the Japanese Society for the Science of Design and the Japan Design Committee. Critic Masaru Katsumie played a critical role in setting these up and laying the foundations of modern Japanese design, alongside key designers such as Isamu Kenmochi, Sōri Yanagi and Riki Watanabe.

By the 1970s, Japanese designers were finding ways to combine traditional aesthetic concepts with new high-tech products and modern materials. The emergence of architects such as Kenzō Tange, Toyo Ito and Tadao Ando gave rise to a number of Japanese architectural movements that acknowledged international modernism while

▲ *Mid-century modern design owes much to Japanese minimalism and its focus on clean lines.*

pursuing their own distinct perspective. Working with concrete, steel and glass, their projects fused contemporary innovation with elements of Japanese traditional design, such as Ando's focus on harmony with a building's natural environment.

From national to international

With its emphasis on simplicity and organic materials, attention to detail, and close connection to nature, traditional Japanese style has influenced much of modern design. From the austere

aesthetic of 1920s Bauhaus to the clean lines of mid-1950s Scandinavian style and the pared-back nature of 1990s minimalism, Japanese aesthetics aligned smoothly with 20th-century design in the West. The ability to fuse old and new, form and function, has ensured a reverence for contemporary Japanese design around the world.

Creativity within constraint

Japan has long led the way in the art of living well in small spaces: driven by necessity as well as design, Japanese homes tend to be compact. Architects have risen to the challenges of designing with constraints to create ingenious spaces, drawing on long-standing principles to connect contemporary Japanese design to its artistic and craft traditions. Natural light, materials in their raw form and views to the outside natural world are achievable for even the smallest space.

Today, Japan is known for its contemporary architecture, with many eye-catching and innovative buildings, large and small. The ability of Japanese design to balance apparent contradictions within itself – to borrow from the West while honouring its indigenous traditions, to reject ornament and yet embrace detail, to fuse craftsmanship with industrial production – continues to be a great strength, enabling it to be flexible and open to change.

The philosophies behind the style

The following concepts, both traditional and modern, are part of a set of aesthetics that have shaped Japanese ideas of taste and beauty, and are seen as hugely important to everyday life and design.

Ma

An essential principle behind Japanese style, *ma* refers to negative space, literally and figuratively. It doesn't mean that something is 'empty', but rather almost the opposite: a space that is open, that can be dynamic. In design terms, *ma* refers to the way in which living spaces can be expanded or contracted by using moveable walls and screens, or the practice of storing away functional furniture when not in use to make rooms feel more open.

Mono no aware

Often depicted as an essential component of Japanese culture, *mono no aware* refers to the deep emotions that objects can evoke in us. It is about an awareness of impermanence – the understanding that all things are transient, that pleasure and sadness are poignantly intertwined. The fleeting nature of beautiful things is integral to their beauty: think of a sunset or the colour of autumn leaves. Japanese aesthetics involve an acceptance and appreciation of natural change.

Wabi

The sense of understated beauty is a foundation of Japanese design. In the *wabi* aesthetic, damaged objects can be seen as more valuable

▸ *The subtle beauty of this branch with its leaves slowly dropping, balanced by the aged, textured pot, is an example of wabi-sabi.*

▸▸ *Leaving plenty of space around your furniture (ma) helps to make a room feel open and inviting.*

than ostensibly unblemished ones, providing they have been repaired well. It implies moderation in all forms, avoiding opulence in favour of elegant simplicity.

Sabi

The beauty of ageing, referring to the Japanese appreciation of natural materials that have weathered and changed over time. *Sabi* evokes plainness, simplicity and asymmetry. The term has been combined with *wabi* to form one principle, *wabi-sabi*, which represents perhaps the most characteristic feature of traditional Japanese beauty. Meaning 'perfect in its imperfections', in design terms *wabi-sabi* translates to distressed woods, aged stone and washed-out natural colours.

Yūgen

Hard to translate precisely, *yūgen* is about grace and subtlety, and the way in which deeper meanings can be suggested rather than explicitly revealed. *Yūgen* can be seen in the sublime simplicity of Japanese contemporary architecture, and its serene yet strong aesthetic that is unmistakably Japanese.

Iki

Broadly summarized as refined yet unpretentious style, *iki* can also be hard to pin down. But according to the philosopher Shūzō Kuki, it has clear application in the world of design: parallel lines, particularly vertical stripes; certain shades of grey, blue and brown; and dim lighting, either from indirect sunlight or paper lanterns.

Embracing nature: inside and out

▲ *Full-length glass doors and windows bring the outside world in.*

In traditional Japanese houses, the line between interior and exterior is a soft one: verandas, big windows and moveable screens open houses out to the garden and draw nature into the home. The garden is intended to be seen from inside the house and is designed accordingly.

Japanese gardens are calm, restful spaces, intended to encourage reflection and meditation. There are many different types, including tea gardens (*chaniwa*) and highly stylized dry gardens (*karesansui*). They use plants carefully to mark the changing seasons, and often feature contrasting textures, such as smooth stones, rough rocks, swirled sand and shiny ceramic containers. They are generally sparsely planted and the space around the plants is as significant as the plants themselves.

▲ *Traditional Japanese houses have an engawa (see page 34) – a veranda or strip of hardwood flooring around the outer edge. It connects the outside world with the house and helps to regulate its temperature during the different seasons.*

▲ A large picture window looking out to the garden frames the view and makes the exterior feel like part of the interior.

▶ Bonsai trees need a lot of care but the rewards are great: they are more like works of art than plants in some ways.

Adding plants with leaves in a range of different colours and textures will evoke the impression of a Japanese garden. Evergreens give year-round colour that is soothing and timeless, while a range of shades adds depth and contrast. Below are some of the plants and trees commonly found in Japanese gardens:

- Bonsai: miniature trees that are pruned and trained to mimic mature trees. Indoor varieties are also available.
- Maple: particularly good for its fiery autumn colour when the leaves glow.
- Flowering cherry: the ultimate symbol of spring, ornamental cherry trees will mark the changing seasons beautifully.
- Azaleas: classically Japanese, these trumpet-shaped spring flowers brighten up a garden with shades of pink, yellow, red and white.
- Black mondo grass: technically not a grass, this has low-growing black foliage, making it great for contrast against brighter plants.
- Moss: commonly seen in Japanese gardens, often in different shades of green.
- Hosta: perfect for shady glens, hostas come in a range of shades, shapes and sizes.

Avoid anything too straight or symmetrical: you want natural, winding shapes that echo organic forms. And small is beautiful – even the tiniest space works well as a Japanese garden!

If you don't have a garden, you can still bring the sense of a traditional Japanese garden into your home. Camellia, umbrella tree, weeping fig and European fan palm all work well as house plants. Colourful floral displays aren't common in Japan, so stick to simple, natural, green arrangements.

▲ *This sunken plant is a dramatic focal point and a great way to bring nature into the room.*

You can also incorporate elements of Japanese style particularly well in small outdoor spaces, such as balconies and window boxes. Try filling stone containers with water and a single plant – a water lily or iris would work well. Collect stones in a range of shades from off-white to grey and brown. Carefully chosen pieces of driftwood can look like sculptural forms worthy of display.

Leaders and icons

In Japanese homes, architecture and interior design combine to create a simple, functional and minimalist aesthetic. Below are some of the major Japanese architects and designers who have pioneered and developed modern Japanese style, combining traditional elements with contemporary materials, and fusing East and West in innovative ways.

Masaru Katsumie (1909–83) A key figure in the development of modern Japanese design post-1945, Katsumie was an influential design critic, teacher and writer, and founded a number of significant design institutions in Japan, such as the Japan Design Committee and the Japanese Society for the Science of Design. He also promoted a greater understanding of Western modernist design to Japan, bringing a Bauhaus exhibition to Tokyo's national art museum in 1954.

Kazuhide Takahama (1930–) After designing the Japanese Pavilion for the Milan Triennale in 1957, Takahama began designing for Gavina SpA, including storage and shelving systems and later soft seating such as the Suzanne Lounge Chair range, which is now produced by Knoll. He pioneered the use of block polyurethane foam seating in the late 1950s and his designs fused Japanese and Western design principles to create clean, modern, yet timeless furniture.

Arata Isozaki (1931–) Initially influenced by modernism, Isozaki has become known as one of Japan's most creative modern architects, particularly for the way his work synthesizes Eastern and Western elements. His innovative structures include the Civic Center for Tsukuba in Ibaraki, Osaka and the Museum of Contemporary Art in Los Angeles.

Shiro Kuramata (1934–91) An architect by training, Kuramata went on to become an interior designer, designing hundreds of bars and restaurants as well as furniture. He established his own design company in 1965 and became instantly famous in 1977 for his 'Drawer in an Irregular Form', redesigning the conventional chest of drawers with undulating curves to give it new life. His creations often subverted the ordinary and have become 20th-century classics, including the 'How High the Moon' chair, made of steel mesh, and the sculptural Revolving Cabinet he designed for Cappellini.

Tadao Ando (1941–) A self-taught architect, Ando's style emphasizes negative space, representing the beauty of simplicity. His buildings are complex while appearing simple, following natural forms in structure and emphasizing sensation and physical experience. He tends to work with large blocks of concrete, which in his designs take on a clean, almost silk-like appearance. In 1995, he won the Pritzker Prize, considered the highest distinction in architecture. He is also known for his creative use of natural light, such as in the Church of the Light in Ibaraki, Osaka.

'I do not believe architecture should speak too much. It should remain silent and let nature in the guise of sunlight and wind speak.' – Ando

Shigeru Uchida (1943–2016) Uchida's designs encompassed furniture, interior design, architecture and urban planning, and he features in collections at the Metropolitan Museum of Art in New York, the San Francisco Museum of Modern Art, and the Conran Foundation, among others. He designed lamps and chairs as well as tea rooms and shop interiors, including a series of boutiques for fashion designer Yohji Yamamoto. His minimalist approach can be seen in his later work for Japanese lighting brand Yamagiwa and his Khora furniture collection, which drew on Japanese scenery for inspiration.

Naoto Fukasawa (1956–) One of the most highly regarded product designers working today, Fukasawa has won multiple awards for his restrained creations that are easy to use. His acclaimed wall-mounted CD player for Muji exemplified his belief that products should be instinctively functional, without needing thought from the user. His designs include lighting for Yamagiwa and Artemide, and furniture and accessories for B&B Italia, Maruni and Driade.

Tokujin Yoshioka (1967–) Before establishing his own company in 2000, Yoshioka studied under Shiro Kuramata and created interiors for fashion designer Issey Miyake. He has won many international design awards and his work is displayed in museums around the world. His delicate and elegant designs combine practicality with poetry, surprising and delighting in equal measure. His Panna chair adapts to the user, while his Honey-Pop chair blends new and old technology by using wafer-thin paper in a honeycomb structure.

Oki Sato (1977–) Canadian–Japanese architect Oki Sato's firm Nendo is one of the world's most exciting young design companies. Prolific in output, they have designed lights for Oluce and furniture for Swedese and De Padova. *Nendo* means 'clay' in Japanese and Sato's intention was for his company to be as flexible as its namesake. The laser-cut ribbon stool he designed for Cappellini combines structural stability with a fluid, playful aesthetic as the pieces of metal loop around each other.

▲ *The Dream Chair, designed by Tadao Ando, is made of heat-moulded three-dimensional plywood and was created as a tribute to designer Hans J. Wegner.*

2. ACHIEVING THE LOOK

Welcome to the Japanese home

▲ *Built-in storage helps you keep your home free of clutter.*

Japan is a country of contradictions, always able to contain two seemingly contrasting elements: traditional and modern, East and West, austere and decorative, monochrome and colourful, playful and serious. Modern Japanese interiors contain elements of traditional and contemporary design, balancing Eastern and Western influences, borrowing what is needed from elsewhere but modifying it to create new forms that feel distinctively Japanese. In this section, we'll look at how these aspects of contrast and balance can be applied when creating your own interiors.

Setting the tone

The most important thing to think about when designing your own home is the overall mood you want to create. Japanese interiors are valued for their calmness and serenity, providing sanctuary from a busy world. In keeping with Zen philosophy, you want to create a calming, enriching space that is designed to go with, not against, nature. Details are subtle but all-important: decor is deliberately understated, but everything should have a place and a purpose. Using bare, natural materials like wood and paper will give your home a calm, harmonious feel.

Multi-tasking rooms

In traditional Japanese houses, rooms had more than one use; a room could change function (and size) throughout the day as needed. Instead of being supported by walls, Japanese wood-framed houses had pillars and moveable partitions that allowed residents to create different spaces. In modern houses, open-plan designs can achieve a similar effect. Screens and folding doors can open or divide spaces for different uses, while full-length sliding glass doors opening to the outdoors help to merge interior and exterior.

Seeing the light

Light sources were traditionally kept low to the ground, in keeping with the custom of sitting on the floor. For Japanese-inspired lighting, try fixing *shōji*-like panels in front of wall-mounted lights, or use paper or opaque glass lanterns. You want soft filtered light that complements the natural colours of your space.

'More with less' living

Traditionally, Japanese rooms look quite bare to Western eyes, with furniture moved around as needed and decoration kept to a minimum. This is particularly practical in small spaces: thinking about how you can do 'more with less' is a great way to evaluate how best to use the space you have. Floor-to-ceiling wall closets are an effective way to store anything that doesn't need to be out on display, and can be designed with opaque sliding doors to mirror *shōji* panels. Futon mattresses double up as seating in the daytime or can be stored away completely. Choose your furniture carefully and bear in mind that the space around each item is just as important as the piece itself: cramming too much into a room will make it feel cluttered and stressful.

◄ *This room includes many of the traditional Japanese pieces of furniture, including a* chabudai *table, but the modern wall and floor finishes give the room a contemporary twist.*

Colour palette

In keeping with the desire to be close to nature, the typical Japanese interior colour palette is pulled from the muted, subdued shades of the natural elements traditionally used in house building and design (see page 30). Opt for matt textures and neutral, subtle shades – creamy whites and browns rather than stark white or black, or earthy light greens and greys inspired by the natural hues of wood and stone.

Shibui

Like *wabi* and *sabi*, *shibui* or *shibusa* is a complex aesthetic. In a general sense it refers to a feeling of refined and unobtrusive beauty: a *shibui* object combines simple design with subtle detail, thus balancing simplicity with complexity.

In interior design, *shibui* colours are earthen and subdued, with grey added to them to create a silvery effect. This ensures a co-ordinated scheme where colours are tied together, and can range from pastel hues to darker shades depending on how much grey is added. Sometimes a brighter colour can be introduced as a highlight for impact, but keep it focused and limited to one or two shades. Darker colours should be closer to the ground and lighter tones higher up on walls or ceilings to reflect nature.

Bringing nature in

The desire to be close to nature means that green is an important colour in Japanese design. It can be added by bringing in plants and flowers or, by moving doors and using windows to frame views, the house caened up to the outside world. *Tatami* mats (see page 38) provide a light green rush floor covering that is also fragrant, like freshly cut hay.

Colour for impact

Lacquer is a distinctively Japanese surface, lustrous and beautiful as well as practical. The dramatic deep dark red and black shades of traditional lacquerware stand out beautifully against the more neutral backgrounds of Japanese interior design.

The call of the ocean

The sea has had a big influence on Japanese art, and blue is more commonly associated with Japanese painting than interior decor, though that doesn't mean it can't be used. Lighter shades will work well as neutrals; darker tones will go better with white, green or yellow decor.

◄ *This internal screen panel uses a map print instead of plain paper or glass for a personalized take on Japanese style.*

▲ *Ikebana, or the Japanese art of flower arranging, involves using as few stems as possible and arranging them asymmetrically to best highlight their natural beauty.*

Materials

Wood, bamboo, paper, straw and stone are the building blocks of traditional Japanese design: originally chosen for practical reasons, they also give Japanese houses their distinctive look and provide a link to the past that is still apparent today. The raw materials themselves are seen as beautiful: their natural properties are appreciated, not disguised or covered up, and they help to make Japanese houses feel connected to nature.

Nonetheless, Japanese style is not dependent on using traditional materials; cement, glass, iron and steel are common in contemporary Japanese architecture. What matters is not the surface in and of itself, but rather the quality of the space created. It is perfectly possible to cultivate the sense of a traditional home using modern furniture or materials.

Bamboo

Used for ceilings and rafters in traditional farmhouses, bamboo is also employed for external blinds. Its durability and flexible nature means it is hugely versatile as a sustainable material for building with. With its smooth, glossy surface, it is beautiful, and is much used decoratively.

Wood

Most Japanese houses are built on timber frameworks, drawn from Japan's pine, cedar and cypress trees. The abundance and range of timber available has ensured a deep appreciation of wood and its warmth, texture and natural irregularity. Cedar is often used for bath tubs in traditional Japanese homes because it is water-resistant and fragrant, bringing the natural world into the bathroom.

Paper (*washi*)

Soft, opaque, handmade rice paper was traditionally used for *shōji* (screens used inside and out) and the heavier *fusuma* (sliding panels that also function as walls and doors) to let diffused

◄ *The* engawa *(see page 34) is an in-between space, part of the house yet also connected to the outside world through light and exposure to the elements.*

▲ Bamboo leaves are silhouetted through the light paper panels of this shōji screen.

◄ Exposed wooden beams and concrete surfaces might seem industrial rather than Japanese, but can work surprisingly well.

▼ The textures and colours of natural stone and wood complement each other beautifully.

light into a room, creating a calm, serene atmosphere. Opaque glass is widely used nowadays where paper isn't practical. Paper lampshades keep artificial light subdued, while paper lanterns give off a lovely warm glow.

Stone

Generally used for exteriors rather than inside, stone is commonly found in paths, entrances and gardens. Like wood, its irregularity is prized, and it glows beautifully in the light of the sun or a lantern. In Japanese rock or Zen gardens, stones are carefully chosen for their individual shape, colour and texture, each contributing to the garden's artistic meaning.

Japanese style elements

Screening devices and partitions

The spatial characteristics of a traditional Japanese house are the horizontal components of floor and roof rather than the vertical structures of (heavy) brick and stone walls. Contrary to houses elsewhere that are composed as an aggregate of individual rooms, the Japanese house is perceived as a one-room space partitioned by only a series of light compartments.

▲ *Originally* shōji *were covered with paper, but nowadays opaque glass is common.*

Shōji

Adopted from aristocratic dwellings, *shōji* is a generic term that refers to sliding partitions made of a latticework wooden or bamboo frame. While there exist many different types, the English connotation commonly refers to a translucent type of sliding screen filled with rice paper, that can act as a room divider, window or door.

Fusuma

A type of *shōji*, *fusuma* are opaque sliding screens made of vertical rectangular panels placed in the interior of a house. Like translucent *shōji*, they are meant to redefine a larger open living area into smaller rooms, and as such create cupboards, function as closet doors or become an internal door.

Byōbu

Originally from China, *byōbu* are folding screens consisting of several frames or panels that are connected by hinges or by other means. This piece of stand-alone furniture had the practical function of preventing drafts inside the house as well as providing residents with a sense of privacy. Richly decorated, they are works of art in their own right.

Sudare

Sudare are rattan blinds that originally replaced the translucent paper sliding screens during the hot and humid Japanese summers. Besides creating shade while allowing a breeze through the house, *sudare* can also serve as dividers to provide privacy or mark a territory.

◀ Sudare *provide privacy without shutting out natural light.*

▼ *These detailed latticework* shōji *frame the view of the garden beautifully.*

Transitional Spaces

A common feature of traditional Japanese architecture is the sense of continuity between inside and outside. A variety of architectural features emphasizes this ambiguity, whereas the transition from exterior to interior becomes a gradual experience.

▲ *When visiting someone's home in Japan it is considered polite to leave your shoes either on the floor, facing the door, or in a specially designated storage space.*

Genkan

Upon entering a Japanese house, one arrives in a small entrance hallway, or *genkan*, used for the removal of shoes. Contrary to the main part of the house that is slightly lifted off the ground, the *genkan* is located on ground level and often contains a shoe rack for storing footwear.

Agarikamachi

The entrance sill, or *agarikamachi*, demarcates the transition from outdoor to indoor by means of a slight height difference. This piece of wood is situated at the threshold of the entry hall. After removing one's shoes in the *genkan*, one steps up the *agarikamachi* to enter the shoeless territory of the actual house.

Doma

Originating in folk dwellings as an intermediate space between the public, external space and private family space, the *doma* is an earthen floor just behind the main entrance. Much larger than the average contemporary *genkan*, this entrance area traditionally functioned like a covered yard for household chores such as cooking, on a bare earthen floor.

Engawa

An edging strip of wood or bamboo flooring running on the outside of the building and partly or completely exposed to the weather, the *engawa* is regarded as an extension of the dwelling space ambiguously situated between the interior and the exterior. Nowadays, the *engawa* often refers to a veranda-like space that is either partly inside the building, with sliding doors protecting it from rain, or completely exposed.

▲ This dramatic entryway uses light to make a statement: keeping the room almost entirely free of furniture or accessories allows you to focus on the contrasting textures of the walls and floors, illuminated by the lantern.

◄ Traditional Japanese homes have a sunken tiled area in the entryway where shoes are left – the step up to the main floor helps to keep dirt out of the house.

▸ *A traditional* furo *should be deep enough to immerse your whole body in.*

▸▾ *A cast-iron kettle (*tetsubin*) is hung over the traditional* irori*.*

▲ *A tokonoma.*

Symbolic elements

Features characteristic of Japanese residential architecture often carry a symbolic or ceremonial meaning, either referring to religious practices or as part of a domestic ritual.

Kamidana

Literally a 'god-shelf', *kamidana* refers to a small household altar to worship the deities of the Shinto faith. Placed high on a wall, the altar contains symbolic objects that refer to the different deities. Worship includes a ritual cleansing of the hands, prayers in front of the altar and the offering of food such as rice, water and fruits.

Tokonoma

Translated as 'alcove room', the *tokonoma* is a *tatami*-clad area in the Japanese living space, the size of one *tatami* mat, specially designated for aesthetic appreciation. It displays a seasonal arrangement containing a hanging scroll, an art object and/or a flower arrangement that has been carefully selected by the host.

Irori

Irori is a type of sunken hearth used for heating the home as well as cooking food. Essentially a square pit excavated in the floor with a cooking pot or kettle on a moveable hook above it, this open hearth is found in both kitchens and the main living space. As an everyday place around which meals were eaten and guests entertained, the *irori* formed the symbolic heart of a commoner's dwelling.

Furo

Honorifically called *ofuro*, the bath tub is an essential part of a bathing ritual. Since the actual cleansing of the body occurs in a separate area in front of the bath, the hot water in the tub is ultimately used for soaking, relaxing and warming the body. While originally made from wood, the modern *furo* is entirely made of acrylic, though the traditional bathing ritual remains essentially the same.

▸ *This simple* chabudai *has particularly slight legs to give it a delicate silhouette.*

▸ *Heavy woven fabric on these* zabuton *cushions makes them hardwearing as well as beautiful to look at.*

Moveable furniture

The floor is the most important surface in Japanese architecture and is used for sitting, squatting and sleeping. From this floor-sitting habit, furniture items developed differently from those of chair-sitting cultures. It was only in the early 19th century that Western-style furniture like high dining tables and high chairs were introduced. Contemporary houses in Japan are often a mix of both cultures.

Tatami

Tatami is a rectangular mat made of tightly woven grass and straw, and since ancient times has been used as a floor covering in traditional Japanese homes. To protect the delicate mats, shoes are removed before entering any *tatami*-covered floor. Its standardized size, roughly 90 by 180 cm, has become a modular unit in Japanese architecture to measure the size of a room and has defined the height of sliding partitions.

Chabudai

The short-legged *chabudai* table forms an essential feature in the floor-sitting lifestyle. It can be used as a family dining table around which people sit to eat, or as a study desk. Its collapsible legs make it easy to store in a closet at night to make room for futon mattresses to sleep on.

Zabuton

To make sitting or kneeling on a *tatami* floor more comfortable, people use flat floor cushions called *zabuton*. The cushions are usually rectangular in size and, like the *chabudai*, are easy to move to another location in the house.

Kotatsu

As Japanese houses are traditionally made to bear the summer heat, winters can be quite harsh. To keep warm, a type of brazier was introduced that replaces the *chabudai* in winter. The *kotatsu* looks like a short-legged table covered with a thick blanket and is equipped with a heater. People sit with legs and lower body under the blanket to stay warm, making the *kotatsu* an embodiment of family togetherness.

▲ *A* kotatsu *is great for eating, drinking, talking or playing games when it's cold outside.*

◄ *The underneath of a* kotatsu.

3. A ROOM-BY-ROOM GUIDE

ENTERING

The entryway

▲ If your entryway is small, using the same colour for walls, floor and ceiling will make it feel more spacious.

▶ Leave plenty of space around your tokonoma so that it doesn't feel cluttered.

The distinction between outside and inside, public and private, is an important one in Japan. Moving from one to another is considered significant, and there are various ways in which that is marked in Japanese homes. The main one is the *genkan*, or Japanese entryway. Something like a porch, lobby, mud room or even a doormat, the *genkan* is generally a small, tiled vestibule or space where you take off your shoes before you enter the house to avoid bringing dirt inside. It can act as an airlock, keeping the inside of the house warm, away from the colder entrance, which is handy, since it is also a place for brief transactions with the outside world, such as receiving deliveries. Beyond its practical purpose, however, it has cultural significance in Japan. In traditional houses, the *genkan* is generally a formal space, and etiquette involves a number of rules about its appearance and usage.

Transitions

Although the *genkan* acts as the interface between the outside world and the private home, the importance of this transition begins with the space around your house. If you have a front exterior area or garden, you could create a sense of crossing in some way, perhaps through a gate, fence, hedge or garden path.

Traditionally, at the entrance to the *genkan* would be a large stone (a *kutsunugi-ishi*), but this has now generally been replaced by a sunken area. This area is where you remove your shoes before stepping up to a wooden platform (*shikidai*) or the main floor of the house. The design is intended to ensure that dirt does not get carried inside: outdoor shoes stay in the *genkan* and both residents and guests can wear slippers (*uwabaki*) inside the house.

be simple – white or neutral shades, natural wood for warmth. You can then display one or two carefully chosen objects, such as a vase, plant or flower arrangement, to adorn the room. (For example, Taku Omura's Ripple vase on page 184 would fit well.) Keeping items of decoration to a minimum encourages guests to properly look at and appreciate them rather than being visually overwhelmed.

Traditionally, a *genkan* would have had an alcove, or *tokonoma*, in which to display a treasured item such as a scroll or flower arrangement (*ikebana*). You can recreate the sense of this dedicated space by using a shelf or the top of a sideboard or table, but be careful not to let it end up as a place for keys, mail or general clutter. Designate somewhere else to put such items – preferably out of sight in a drawer or cupboard. If you have limited space, try hanging a picture instead. Images of nature in particular will help to inculcate the sense of closeness to the natural world that is so important to Japanese design.

A doorway from the *genkan* to the rest of the house further emphasizes its usage as a transitional space.

An interpretation of the *genkan* might be that it is a place where, along with outerwear, you can leave behind the stresses of daily life before entering the sanctuary of home. As such, it should feel welcoming but not too personal a space.

Decoration

The *genkan* represents what you show of your home to visitors, and as such it's vital to make it an attractive area. In keeping with Japanese design principles, this is best achieved by keeping your entryway as clear as possible. Decor should

Storage

The Japanese entryway doesn't need to contain much in the way of furniture, but some form of storage is essential. Guests don't need to use it, but a *getabako*, or antique shoe cabinet, will help you keep the space clear and organized. Whether stored away or not, it's customary to position shoes with the toes facing the door. If you have room, consider installing a cupboard that will let you shut away coats, umbrellas, sports equipment and any other outerwear. Alternatively, use wall hooks to store coats and jackets, and an umbrella rack for wet-weather gear. (See the Yamazaki umbrella stand on pages 62–3 for a good example of the latter.)

◄◄ *Open-faced shelving such as this sideboard can be a great way to combine storage with a space to display accessories.*

◄ *Entryways are not just for storing shoes. With open shelving such as this, you can store favourite or useful objects to create a welcoming space.*

Try searching antiques galleries for shoe cabinets if you want a traditional piece. If something more modern would be a better fit for your home, retailers such as Muji or Habitat offer clean, simple storage solutions in a range of materials. Wood is always a good choice, but steel or a natural material like rattan will also work well.

Floor

In contemporary houses and apartments, space is often limited, and the entryway may well lead off or be part of another room. If this is the case, one way to delineate the *genkan* space is to use a different type of flooring there. Tiling is a great and traditional way to set the space apart, but you could also use a different kind of wood or laminate flooring from the rest of your home, or any sort of hard floor if the rest of your space is carpeted. More simply, a large mat or rug would work to give a sense of the *genkan* as a separate area.

Case study

Designer/Owner Mata Design Studio > **Year(s)** 2018 > **Place** Perth, Australia

The *genkan* or hallway is a hugely important space: the entrance point to a house, it acts as the interface between the public space and the private family home. It is where you receive guests and interact with tradespeople, and so it needs to be presentable as well as functional. This stunning *genkan* is a luxuriously large room by most standards, but the principles underpinning its design are universal regardless of size.

In this room, each family member has their own cupboard for storing coats, bags and other outerwear: all that storage space helps to keep the room completely free of clutter. The simple cupboard design emphasizes oak's natural grain and beauty without unnecessary ornament.

The marble plinth to the right signifies the transition from the *genkan* to the rest of the house and is deliberately made from a different material to the main floor to symbolize the distinction. It also has a practical use: inside is a hidden shoe drawer.

This lovely, light-filled space makes full use of skylights and a full-length window to flood the room with plenty of natural daylight, while targeted spotlights provide additional lighting as needed. The neutral white decor keeps things simple and lets you focus on the beauty of the natural wood floor and cupboards with no distraction.

Plants *Grouping together plants of different sizes and in different containers is a simple way of creating an attractive arrangement. Asymmetry is a key component of Japanese style.*

Decoration *As the* genkan *is where you receive your guests, it's common to decorate it with artwork or a floral arrangement. Here the single piece of art is displayed effectively against the white wall, its landscape subject matter another means of bringing nature into the room.*

Shoe storage *The* genkan *generally has a cabinet for storing shoes (a* getabako*). Here the shoes have been neatly hidden away in a concealed shoe drawer built into the plinth, which also contains slippers for residents and guests entering the house.*

Floor *Traditionally, the* genkan *floor is concrete or tiled, though this wooden floor is a great choice, imbuing warmth and colour to the room.*

Signature colours

This hallway is an excellent example of the way contrasting textures are used to good effect in Japanese-style homes. The wallpaper has been designed to look like a richly painted screen, using traditional motifs and warm, luxurious colours to create an oriental feel. The black vertical lines and lustrous finish mimic the sensuous texture of silk-panelled screens, while the images of the natural world link the room to the outdoors. It's a clever way to use wallpaper, which is not commonly found in Japanese homes, and works best when used sparingly: stick to one wall or alcove rather than covering a whole room.

Black furniture works very well against this wall, and the laquered table provides both storage and a space to display objects. Its glossy surface is a nice contrast against the heavier texture of the wallpaper and also with the rug, which minimizes dirt coming into the house and also provides warmth. Its neutral tones are deliberately low-key.

The crackleware vase is yet another textural contrast, its delicate monochrome pattern providing horizontal lines that sit in classic juxtaposition to the ones seen in the wallpaper and rug. The cotton branch matches the vase with its dark stem and white cotton balls, adding a delicate softness and another touch of nature. The light and shadows cast against the wall and floor add another dimension to the space.

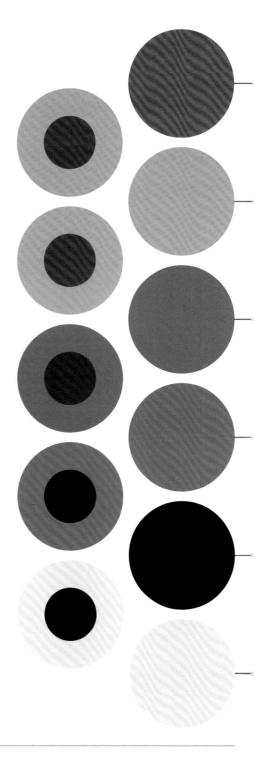

Ishinomaki bench

On 11 March 2011, the most powerful earthquake ever recorded in Japan triggered a devastating forty-metre-high tsunami that hit the northern coastal region of Tōhoku, travelling as far as ten kilometres inland near Sendai, the second largest city north of Tokyo.

In the aftermath of the disaster, as one of many incentives designed to help rehabilitate the lives of those affected by the devastation, a furniture workshop was founded in Ishinomaki, a coastal city north of Sendai. Ishinomaki Laboratory began running simple DIY workshops for local people, and one of the first projects involved the creation of over forty benches for a temporary outdoor cinema space.

These simple benches, initially offered free of charge, were extremely popular with residents and subsequently became the first commercial product for the Ishinomaki Laboratory brand, which now markets products beyond the local community. Designed primarily for outdoor use, the benches are perfect for gardens or patios and create a warm, rustic feel for interior spaces.

Designer
Keiji Ashizawa

Source
Ishinomaki Laboratory

Material
Red cedar

Dimensions
Width: 150 cm
Depth: 32 cm
Height: 42 cm

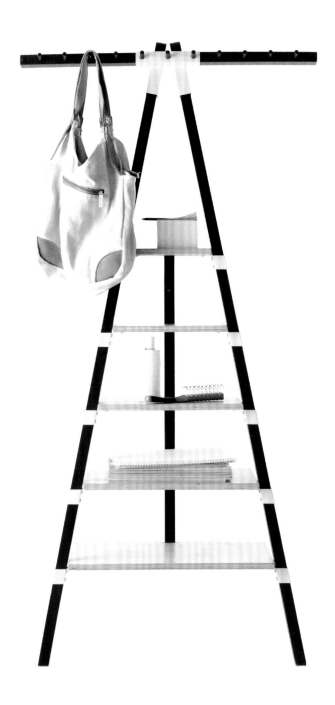

IKEA PS wall shelf

Keiji Ashizawa (see also pages 54–5) was commissioned by Swedish retail giant IKEA to create this unique storage and display piece for their PS collection. All the items in the PS collection are designed to be flexible, portable and space-saving, and are aimed primarily at younger professionals who might rent small apartments and are likely to relocate relatively often. The leaning A-frame construction of the PS shelf means the unit does not need to be fixed with screws or brackets – rentals often forbid tenants from drilling holes in the walls.

The design consists of five birch plywood shelves fixed with steel brackets to a solid birch frame – something of a departure from the laminated chipboard furniture IKEA is famous for. The horizontal hanging rack with its eleven pegs adds stability to the frame, making it practically impossible for the unit to topple sideways. The rack also allows the unit to be placed in a corner, providing further space-saving options.

Designer
Keiji Ashizawa

Source
IKEA

Material(s)
Solid birch, birch plywood, steel

Dimensions
Width: 47 cm
Depth: 36 cm
Height: 110 cm

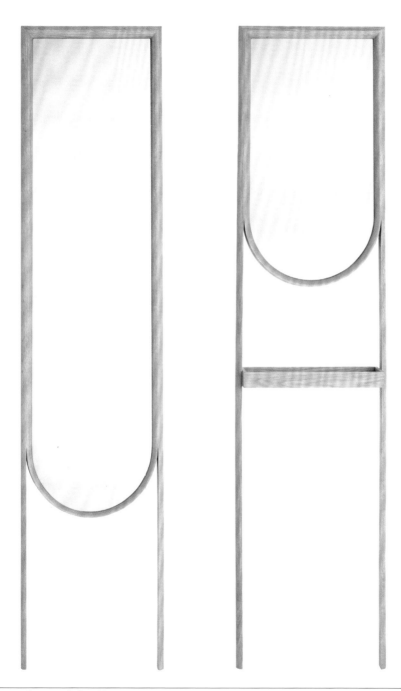

Splinter mirror

The splinter mirror is part of a larger collection of pieces that also includes a chair, a coat stand and a side table. All the pieces in the collection were designed by Nendo for Conde House, a manufacturer based in the Asahikawa region, an area of Japan famous for wooden furniture production.

Manufacturing utilizes a technique that makes the various components appear as though they were peeled away from the thicker wooden stems of each piece of furniture, which provide structural strength. This is achieved by splitting (or splintering) the wood, and the end result rather resembles the way bark peels away from the branch of a tree.

As is the case with many Japanese-influenced pieces, the splinter mirror is designed to lean against a wall, so does not require any fixing. It is offered in two options: one with a full-length mirror; and another that incorporates a small boxed shelf mounted between the legs.

Design
Nendo

Source
Conde House

Material
Oak

Dimensions
Width: 40 cm
Depth: 3.5 cm
Height: 160 cm

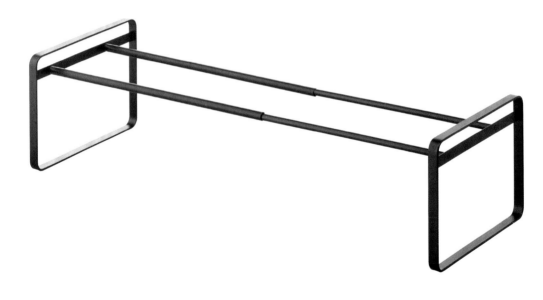

Shoe rack

Yamazaki has been making high-quality homeware products for over one hundred years, after starting out as a small, family-run operation making ironing boards. Its highly regarded products bring a simplicity and intelligence to the kind of everyday items we have in our houses and often take for granted – objects such as dish drainers, umbrella stands, side tables, portable wardrobes and shoe racks.

The company produces a number of self-assembly shoe racks with a variety of configurations. If you have a modest collection of shoes, there is an upright five-pair option that would fit neatly into a narrow space between a pair of cupboards. A few more pairs can be accommodated by the tubular steel low-level rack, arguably the most useful of all the designs as it fits neatly underneath a bed or within the base of a wardrobe, and can be extended outwards to fit up to eight or nine pairs of shoes. The same basic design is also available with a wooden rack replacing the steel tubing.

Design
Yamazaki

Source
Yamazaki

Material(s)
Steel

Dimensions
Width: 70 cm
Depth: 25 cm
Height: 17.5 cm

Smart umbrella stand

Yamazaki don't just make shoe racks (see pages 60–1); the high-quality homeware company that began over one hundred years ago as a small family business manufactures an extensive range of products that are sold worldwide to a discerning clientele wishing to create the perfect Japanese look for their homes.

The Yamazaki smart umbrella stand is a small and compact unit designed to hold up to four umbrellas. This doesn't sound especially smart, as indicated in the name of the product, until you turn the stand around to reveal the adaptable shelf located approximately halfway between the top and bottom of the two-sided case. This simple and neatly concealed device facilitates the storage of both full-size rolled umbrellas and compact folding umbrellas at the same time. The individual square drip trays can be moved to the higher shelf, preventing short umbrellas from falling through to the bottom of the stand.

Design
Yamazaki

Source
Yamazaki

Material(s)
Steel and plastic

Dimensions
Width: 11 cm
Depth: 11 cm
Height: 30 cm

RELAXING

The living room

The living room is generally the most convivial part of the home, where family and guests gather to relax and unwind. During much of the 20th century, the traditional Japanese living room or *ima* was based around the *chabudai*, a small, low table around which people sat with their legs tucked underneath them. These days, sofas and armchairs are much more common but generally furniture in Japan still tends to be lower to the ground.

The *kotatsu* (see page 39) is still commonly used in Japan as a way of staying warm through the winter months, but as Western homes are mostly centrally heated, it's less of an essential. A coffee table is probably more useful, and if it encompasses storage like Atilla Kuzu's sleek and clever Barringer slide table (see pages 76–7), so much the better.

▲ Rather than covering up the natural materials your house is made from, Japanese style favours allowing them to shine: exposed floorboards or plastered walls provide subtle colour and texture. Here the neutral colours of this living room allow the unusual geometric-patterned ceiling to take centre stage.

▶ This room mixes modern pieces with a striking quartet of antique panels. A warm-hued rug on the floor softens the hard lines of this modern space.

Decor

Although simplicity and sparseness of design will always serve you well when it comes to recreating Japanese style, the living room is perhaps the best space when it comes to experimenting with bolder colour and design. Bright colours and prints aren't often suited to Japanese rooms, but the living room might be the exception. A statement wall papered with a Japanese-influenced print or a bold colour could work well if co-ordinated with the rest of the room, or if you would like to work within traditional conventions you could keep walls neutral and instead provide colour and contrast with a piece of art, a multi-panelled screen or even a kimono hung on the wall.

Textural contrast is important in Japanese style, and traditional Japanese wall finishes incorporated elements such as sand or rice straw for their textures. A rougher finish for walls such as stucco, clay plaster or concrete will contrast effectively

A place for everything

Built-in storage is very common in classic Japanese homes, where rooms are seen as flexible and multi-functional and furniture is designed to be portable and brought out as needed. If your room doesn't have built-in cupboards, bookcases, cabinets and sideboards can help your living room feel clear of clutter while also being attractive pieces of furniture in their own right. It's best to start by streamlining your possessions though: you don't want to end up with a room crammed with storage or cupboards that are full to bursting. Ask yourself whether you really need every item: does it have a place or a clear function? If not, that may be a sign that you don't really need it.

Seating

Perhaps surprisingly for a country that traditionally makes only limited use of furniture in its homes, Japan is noted for its contemporary furniture design. Initially influenced by Scandinavian style and European Modernism, designers such as Riki Watanabe, Shigeru Uchida and Shiro Kuramata pioneered an approach that combined Western influences with traditional Japanese values to create a distinctly Japanese approach to seating in particular. Motomi Kawakami's Sestina sofa (see pages 80–1) is rooted in Japan's traditional culture and craftsmanship yet feels timeless and modern. Others have drawn on the more playful side of Japanese design: Toshiyuki Kita's iconic 'Wink' chair is known for its Mickey Mouse ears – a nod to Pop Art aesthetics – as well as its adjustable frame and changeable covers. Still in production today, an investment piece like Kita's playful classic sets the tone for a room and is a great base to build around. Don't discount more simple forms of seating though: floor cushions work well as additional

with a smooth wood floor. Japanese plasters have a subtle lustre and beautiful natural colour, so are a great alternative to paint.

Lighting

Ideally your living room should have plenty of natural daylight flowing through it and a pleasant view to the outside world. If the view isn't up to much, you could use translucent glass or paper screens to obscure it while still allowing daylight in. Curtains aren't typically seen much in Japanese homes, but if you want to use them, go for sheer, gauzy fabrics that won't shut out all the light. Lamps with bright bulbs diffused by paper or obscure glass shades will work better than overhead lighting, and will enable you to provide suitable illumination for different tasks.

seating as you can store them away when not in
use, keeping your room clear.

Screens

If your living room also serves as your dining
room, folding screens or sliding doors will create
a sense of partition between spaces and give you
flexibility as to how your room is used at different
times. Fitting opaque *shōji* panels over cupboard
doors or frames is an easy way to incorporate
Japanese style and can be used to conceal
anything you don't want on permanent display,
such as televisions or sound systems. Though,
given Japan's reputation for innovative and
aesthetically pleasing tech, you may not want to
hide your sleek electronics.

◄ *Paper lanterns give out soft, diffused light
and have the added bonus of looking
attractive, like this sculptural tall shade.*

▲ *The brown Eames chair and contrasting
wooden panelled screen on the mezzanine
level work together to create a calming,
harmonious space.*

Case study

Designer/Owner Richard Smith > **Year(s)** 2017 > **Place** Cape Town, South Africa

This contemporary living room is a great example of how to use colour effectively: the right accessories, carefully chosen, can transform a neutral base and make a room feel fresh and bright. This is a modern take on Japanese style and there is little wood on show, but the custom of allowing raw materials to speak for themselves can still be seen in the bare concrete walls.

The floor-to-ceiling window provides plenty of natural light, while its frame emulates the panelling of a *shōji* screen. The window frames the exterior view beautifully – an important consideration in Japanese homes, where gardens are designed to be seen from inside the house.

The room is furnished with Western pieces such as a sofa and sideboard, but the owners have chosen carefully: the angular furniture and rug provide the vertical and horizontal lines that are so much a feature of traditional Japanese decor. The result is a very modern space that still captures the spirit of Japanese style.

Good use is made of neutral tones – keeping the walls, floor, rug and sofa in plain block colours means the dramatic print really sings, along with pops of colour provided by the floor cushions, ceramic vases and flowers. In keeping with Japanese aesthetics, the artwork has been deliberately positioned asymmetrically: rather than aligning neatly, it is balanced by the sideboard and sofa. The composition is much more dynamic and engaging as a result.

Sideboard *If you don't have built-in cupboard space, a sideboard is an excellent storage option and also provides room to display carefully curated accessories, such as these ceramic vases.*

Drama *With its Japanese motifs, the wall art is a statement piece that works really well in this space – in a very neutral environment it might dominate completely, but here it is balanced by bold colours dotted around the room.*

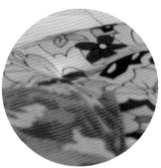

Floor cushions *Practical as well as decorative, these floor cushions add colour and character to the room while providing additional seating that can also be stored away.*

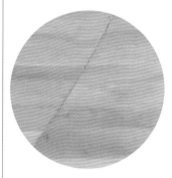

Rug *This simple rug in subtle, earthy shades of beige and taupe reflects the colour of the walls and ties the space together.*

Signature colours

Texture is an important element in Japanese
style and this room shows us how to use it well.
The pale parquet flooring and the distressed wall
– breeze block showing signs of ageing – combine
to form a base palette of soft warm greys and
browns. The grain of the wood and the rough
tone of the breeze block each add depth and
textural interest.

Paring materials back to their essence reveals
the beauty to be found in their raw properties.
Putting them together shows how natural and
synthetic materials can work together harmoniously
and is a reminder that man-made substances can
be just as tactile as natural ones: if you like the
properties of natural stone but baulk at the cost,
breeze block is an excellent affordable alternative!

The daybed sharpens the room up; its clean
lines, warm wood frame and black upholstery
stand out smartly against the wall. Additional
texture is provided by the quilted cushions (the
white and grey ones adding lightness) and the soft
shaggy rug on the floor. Its cream and brown hues
match the floorboards, showing how thoughtfully
this room was put together.

The shadow of the window cast onto the wall
shows how light affects the space: natural daylight
will illuminate its perfect imperfections, while soft
lighting in the evening – provided by this lamp or a
simple candle in a lantern – will create an entirely
different atmosphere.

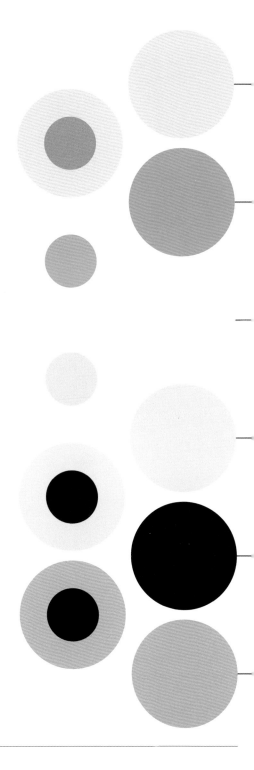

Barringer slide table

The International Furniture Design Fair Asahikawa (IFDA) is a triennial event that has been held since 1990 in Asahikawa, a city on the Japanese island of Hokkaido, famous for the production of wooden furniture. It was at this event in 2002 that the Turkish interior and furniture designer Atilla Kuzu first exhibited this ingenious low-level coffee table. Kuzu is the co-founder of the Istanbul-based architecture and design firm Zoom TPU.

The Japanese compulsion to de-clutter living spaces is served well by the Barringer slide table. The surface of the table is divided into separate quadrants, one of which features a slatted indentation forming a bowl. The three solid quadrants, made from a wood veneer with solid wood edges, can all slide outwards from the centre of the table to reveal storage space beneath. It is the perfect solution for hiding the usual paraphernalia that would otherwise clutter your pristine living room. The table is available in two sizes with two different height options.

Designer
Atilla Kuzu

Source
Zoom TPU

Material(s)
Japanese oak, walnut

Dimensions
Width: 100/120 cm
Depth: 100/120 cm
Height: 20/30 cm

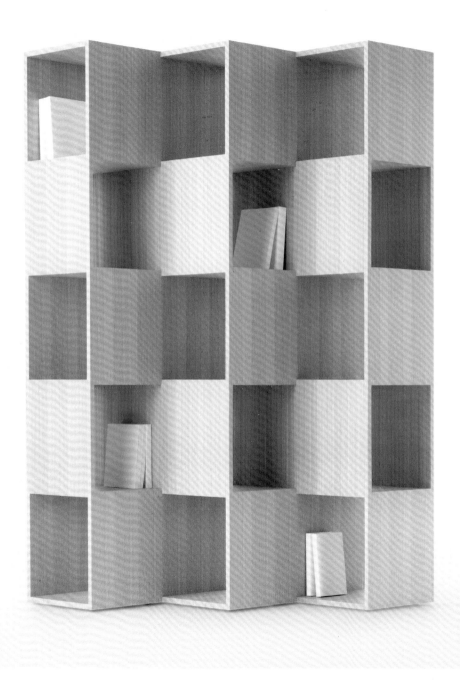

Fold bookshelf

Bookshelves are used as a key feature in living rooms throughout the world and Japanese interiors are no exception. Free-standing shelf units are prevalent in Japanese homes, given the inclination to avoid fixing heavy items to walls. Japanese construction techniques often employ relatively thin, hollow walls (which are safer in areas affected by earthquakes), so don't offer as much support as a thicker stone or block wall.

Designed by the Tokyo-based firm Nendo, the Fold bookshelf is almost illusional in its clever construction. It's made from interlocking wooden boards that are orientated at ninety-degree angles to form a zig-zag shaped series of stacked boxes. The quality of the construction by well-known manufacturer Conde House means the joints look to be completely seamless; single boards appear to have been woven together like a paper chain. As well as a stylish bookcase, the Fold can be used as an effective room divider.

Design
Nendo

Source
Conde House

Material
Oak

Dimensions
Width: Various available widths
Depth: 49 cm
Height: 185 cm

Sestina sofa

A sofa is often one of the largest (and most noticeable) items of furniture in any living room, so it is very important to make the right choice. As with any purchase, it is possible to spend a great deal of money if you are looking for the best quality, and the Sestina sofa, designed by Motomi Kawakami for Conde House, sits somewhere near the higher end in terms of cost. However, you get what you pay for, and those in the Sestina collection (*sestina* can be translated as 'order') are instant classics.

The Sestina sofa is available in two widths and in various finishes. The design is based closely on traditional Japanese lines; the openness of the supporting framework creates a sense of space at floor level and the horizontal wooden base, which is set flush with the seating, acts as a kind of built-in side table.

Designer
Motomi Kawakami

Source
Conde House

Material(s)
Ash / walnut, leather, various fabrics

Dimensions
Width: 210 cm / 240 cm
Depth: 92 cm
Height: 79 cm
Seat height: 41 cm

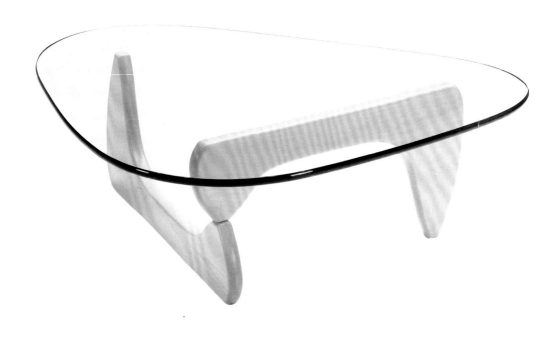

Noguchi coffee table

The Japanese-American industrial designer Isamu Noguchi created the first version of this iconic modernist table in 1939 as a commission for Anson Conger Goodyear, president of New York's Museum of Modern Art. The original rosewood and glass table so impressed the design team at American manufacturer Herman Miller that they asked Noguchi to develop the design into the organic form that we see today, and full production began in 1947.

The IN-50 coffee table (as it is officially named), remained in production until 1973. It was reissued as a limited edition in 1980 before being reintroduced permanently in 1984. The table is so popular that Herman Miller now refers to it simply as 'the Noguchi table'. A genuine Herman Miller table is a relatively expensive purchase, but they are widely available due to the continuing production status. If on a budget, there are acceptable quality reproductions available that are considerably less costly.

Designer
Isamu Noguchi

Source
Herman Miller

Material(s)
Walnut / birch / cherry, glass, aluminium

Dimensions
Width: 128.5 cm
Depth: 92.5 cm
Height: 40 cm

Rin remote control rack

If one were to single out the most important component of a classic Japanese-style interior, it would likely be the absence of clutter. This doesn't mean empty rooms devoid of character, but rather a sense of order where there are no loose items scattered about on coffee tables or sideboards. However, hiding useful and oft-needed items away in drawers and cupboards is not particularly convenient; this is where the Rin remote control rack comes in.

The elegant moulded unit designed by quality homeware manufacturer Yamazaki is constructed from a single piece of plywood shaped into a curve. Two holes, differing slightly in size to accommodate larger and smaller remotes, line up vertically with narrow, horizontal plywood strips attached to the base to stop the remotes slipping backwards or forwards when placed in the unit. The sleek design blends neatly into pretty much any interior but looks particularly comfortable when paired with a wooden coffee table. It is a simple, functional object that does one job well while simultaneously managing to look stylish.

Design
Yamazaki

Source
Yamazaki

Material
Plywood

Dimensions
Width: 15 cm
Depth: 12 cm
Height: 15.5 cm

Sestina Lux media cabinet

A component of the extensive Sestina Lux range of Japanese-influenced furniture offered by Conde House, the Sestina Lux media cabinet is the perfect choice for anyone who dislikes the sight of tangles of wires next to a television or audio system. Available in two widths to suit the dimensions of the room and amount of media equipment to be accommodated, the Tokyo-based designer and educator Motomi Kawakami has managed to combine modern functionality with classic Japanese aesthetics in this piece.

The cabinet can be purchased with the additional option of a built-in infrared relay unit to keep everything even neater, and up to four pieces of audio-visual equipment can be controlled using the signals from their own separate remote units stored inside the cabinet without opening the doors.

Designer
Motomi Kawakami

Source
Conde House

Material(s)
Japanese ash, walnut

Dimensions
Width: 165/220 cm
Depth: 51 cm
Height: 40 cm

Harbor armchair

Naoto Fukasawa has worked with B&B Italia,
the contemporary furniture manufacturer based in
Novedrate, Italy, on a number of key product lines,
including the extensive Papilio series of chairs
and sofas. The Harbor armchairs, high-backed
with a headrest and a lower-backed version,
are something of an extension of Fukasawa's
experiments with the inverted and truncated
cone shape as an ergonomic form for seating.

Both versions of the Harbor armchair have a
particularly cool and highly functional feature: a
built-in swivel base, which makes the chairs highly
manoeuvrable and adaptable for a broad range of
spaces. The covers can be removed completely if
they require cleaning, and fabric choices include a
full-leather option. In addition to the armchairs, a
matching ottoman that aligns neatly with the seat
height of the chairs is available. A separate tray
element can be combined with the ottoman
to convert it into a useful side table.

Designer
Naoto Fukasawa

Source
B&B Italia

Material(s)
Steel, shaped polyurethane, fabric,
leather

Dimensions
Width: 80 cm
Depth: 83/89 cm
Height: 85/104 cm

COOKING

The kitchen

As the kitchen is primarily a utilitarian space, it is important when designing it that form follows function, rather than the other way around. Japanese design naturally follows this principle, but it does so without sacrificing aesthetic considerations: by keeping things simple, you can create a kitchen that works well, looks good and is pleasant to spend time in, whether its purpose is purely functional or also sociable. Above all, there should be a place for everything: if you want to keep something in your kitchen, you need a space to store it.

Storage

Think carefully about what you need to keep in your kitchen and then build in extra storage on top of that: you want to be able to store the majority of your cookware and other items away but, equally, you should be able to access them quickly and easily. Keeping things out on countertops looks messy and means you have less workspace available. Opting for deep drawers rather than cupboards can be a good way to store crockery and bulkier items such as pots and pans, letting you see at a glance what the contents are.

For items you want to keep out on display, open shelves work well without taking up counter space, while wall-mounted storage can be an effective way to organize cooking utensils and other items. Japanese brand Yamazaki (see pages 60–3, 84–5, 110–11) offers a wide range of sleek, fuss-free and affordable organizational products, from dish drainers to towel racks.

Materials

Japanese design favours restraint over opulence, and an appreciation of modest, unadorned interiors rather than those that feel ostentatious or highly

▲ *Wall-mounted storage keeps your counters clear and can also look attractive.*

▶ *A palette of neutrals and greys makes a good backdrop against which you can add pops of colour, as with this kitchen.*

▲ *Open shelves can work really well in a kitchen, if you keep them organized and tidy.*

styled. The intention is to take pleasure in both the raw material and the craftsmanship behind the finished product, whether you opt for natural or synthetic materials.

If you want a natural, 'honest' material such as wood, sustainability is integral: balance is an important consideration in Japanese style, in this case between people and products, nature and the built environment. Bamboo is an environmentally friendly substance that is also typically Japanese and is well worth considering as a flexible, hardwearing flooring option for kitchens.

Concrete, meanwhile, is an elegantly modern, robust choice for countertops, and can also be a good eco option, especially compared with imported stone. Its widespread use in contemporary Japanese architecture makes it a great option for a Japanese-style kitchen.

Doors

The *shibui* aesthetic is worth bearing in mind when designing the Japanese-style kitchen: refined beauty comes from balancing simplicity with subtle detail. Cabinet doors are not the place for detail, however: plain, handle-less cabinet fronts will generally work better than patterned or detailed ones. If you want handles, go for simple clean lines rather than anything ornate. Ensuring that appliances are built in behind cabinet doors will give your kitchen a unified, minimalist look.

Shōji screens are such an iconic symbol of Japanese design that it is worth considering whether they can be used to good effect in your kitchen: if you have an open-plan layout, a free-standing screen can be a flexible way to create a sense of distinction between the kitchen and other parts of the room. Alternatively, using translucent glass inserts on overhead cabinets evokes the feel of a *shōji* screen, particularly when lit from within.

Lighting

Unlike other rooms, overhead lighting may be necessary in the kitchen to ensure that you have proper illumination while cooking. LED strip lights below wall-mounted cabinets or miniature recessed lights within cabinets are a subtle way to provide extra task lighting for work surfaces.

Colour

Traditionally tending towards the monochromatic, Japanese style now has similarities with the Scandinavian sensibility (note the hybrid 'Japandi' design trend of recent years, melding the two) in terms of softening blacks into charcoal and adding warmth to white interiors with greys and soft earthy colours. Stick to simple white crockery and

◄ Handle-less drawers and cabinet
doors work best in a Japanese kitchen.

steel cutlery for minimal dining: you can always
add colour and impact with decorative accessories
such as napkins or serving bowls. Avoid primary
colours or anything too 'shout-y'.

Greening your space

Add a touch of green to your kitchen: a bonsai
tree in a simple ceramic pot will work well, while
garden herbs in planters combine colour and
practical usage. Alternatively, for an effective
but low-key green option, preserved moss needs
almost no maintenance and will give you year-
round colour. Moss is a signature plant in the
Japanese garden, revered for its understated
beauty, sensual texture and longevity: bringing
it into your kitchen helps to invoke a sense of
deep tranquillity and harmony.

Case study

Designer/Owner Andreas von Einsiedel > **Year(s)** 2016 > **Place** Glasgow, Scotland

Given Japan's reputation for compact living, it comes as no surprise that the Japanese kitchen tends to be an efficient, clutter-free space, where everything has its place. Interestingly, regardless of actual size, Japanese-influenced kitchens generally do not feel small or cramped. That is because a lot of thought and care goes into their layout to ensure they feel airy and spacious.

This serene, relaxing kitchen has been designed to be as open as possible, making full use of the space available. The *shōji* screen helps to demarcate the kitchen, but doesn't close it off completely, allowing light through while enabling the inhabitants to adjust the layout according to their needs.

Soft, pale colours and large windows make the space bright and light, while wooden countertops and flooring provide warmth and a link to the natural world outside. Decoration is provided by carefully chosen ceramics, plants and candles in complementary shades, creating a soothing colour palette, while plenty of storage means everything else can be tidied away. The result is a tranquil, harmonious room that feels much larger than it is.

Frame *The large plant frames the room and co-ordinates with the view through the window to draw the natural world in.*

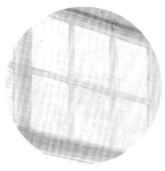

Blinds *Reed or bamboo blinds let you shut out glare while still letting light in. They also fit perfectly with the natural tones in this room.*

Mat *Using a rush or seagrass mat nods to the tatami mat and traditional Japanese style. Their durability and sturdiness make them a great choice for a kitchen.*

Storage *A storage unit on casters is easy to move around, giving you maximum flexibility as well as additional counter space. Open shelves give you the opportunity to display items without cluttering up work surfaces.*

Colour *Soft, complementary colours – cream and white, pale green and blue, the warm tones of wood, paper and reed – work together to make this a calm, soothing environment.*

Drawers *These Shaker-style drawer fronts and drawer knobs aren't typical of Japanese kitchen design, which tends towards flat surfaces and handle-less doors, but they sit well here alongside other more rustic touches such as the fruit bowls.*

Signature colours

Pastel tones aren't the first colours that spring to mind when thinking about Japanese style, but this contemporary kitchen proves that they can work surprisingly well. The trick is to hold to traditional principles in other elements of the room, giving you a solid base from which to experiment with colour. The high-gloss, handle-less kitchen units are typically Japanese, and plentiful storage space means an absence of clutter, invoking a serene and calming atmosphere. Subtle under-cupboard lighting enhances the natural daylight the room receives, while the white ceiling and marble floor provide a neutral backdrop to anchor the coloured cabinets. The patterned ceiling offers an interesting textural contrast to the gleaming floor.

The oak breakfast bar attached to the island counter provides a warm wood base, echoed by the wooden chopping boards on display. The wood effectively grounds the glossy rose pink and pale blue units, which otherwise might feel a little saccharine. Quartz countertops with gold edging add a touch of subtle luxe, which is echoed in the bold ceiling light: a deliberately asymmetric piece that holds its own in this room. The carefully chosen accessories – vases, mirror, bar stools – pick up on the gold finish, tying the room together. The result is a room that feels distinctively Japanese, yet also fresh and unique.

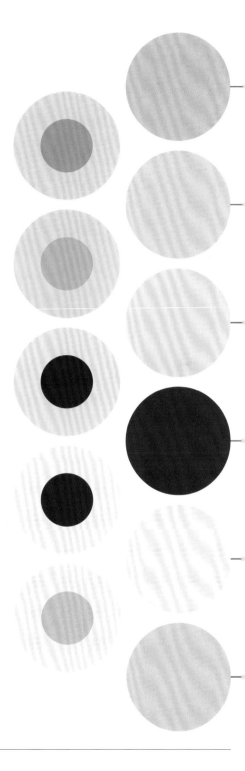

Kamenoko Tawashi scrubbing brush

As the story goes, the young Nishio Shouzaemon yearned to invent a successful new product that would give his family a better life. His first attempt, a hemp palm doormat, was unfortunately unsuccessful; a similar product had already been patented in England. However, one day he noticed that his wife had cut a piece off his doormat to make a scrubbing brush. After some experimentation, Shouzaemon came up with the Kamenoko Tawashi, which translates as 'small turtle scrubber', given its resemblance to a turtle, which also happens to be the symbol for long life in Japan.

This was in 1907, and the product has not changed since it first went into production. The biodegradable brushes are extremely durable, and are a staple in Japanese households where they are used for cleaning just about everything. Found mainly in the kitchen, where they are employed for cleaning pots and utensils, or for scrubbing fresh vegetables, softer versions of the brush – for use in the bathroom – are also available.

Designer
Nishio Shouzaemon

Source
Kamenoko Tawashi Nishio Shoten

Material
Hemp palm

Dimensions
Width: 7 cm
Length: 8.5 / 13 cm

SyuRo brass storage canister

SyuRo is a small retail outlet founded by interior designer Masuko Unayama in 2000, in Torigoe, a district of Tokyo. Her store sells beautifully designed household items inspired by *monozukuri*, a Japanese manufacturing style that revolves around a meticulous dedication to craftsmanship and continuous improvement.

Unayama's inspiration for the store stemmed from a concern that the skills associated with *monozukuri* were being lost due to today's demand for cheaper, mass-market products; SyuRo provides an outlet for artisanal, hand-crafted products that are principally made from tin, brass or copper in a dedicated workshop by local craftsmen. A range of round, metal storage cans is available, including an 8-cm brass jar that is perfect for storing tea. The jars are wonderfully tactile, gradually changing colour over time through oxidization as the natural oils from one's hands react with the brass, and every jar is a unique, one-off piece.

Designer
Masuko Unayama

Source
SyuRo

Material
Brass

Dimensions
Diameter: 7.5 cm
Height: 8 cm

Mayu teapot

Based in Do-Machi, a town in the Japanese prefecture of Yamagata, the Wazuqu workshop of Kikuchi Hojudo is a long-established business that has operated under continuous family ownership (through fifteen generations) since its establishment in 1604. The brand name Wazuqu, used by Kikuchi Hojudo Inc., is based on the word *wazuku,* which is a particular type of cast iron used to make traditional Japanese 'katana' swords. It should be noted that the Mayu teapot is not made of *wazuku*, although the firm do use *wazuku* in the manufacture of a high-end *tetsubin* tea kettle for boiling water directly over a flame.

Their Mayu teapots are prized items crafted to a very high standard. The interiors of the cast-iron pots are finished with enamel, while exteriors are baked with a special paint at a very high temperature to create the rich coloured effect. The refined manufacturing techniques employed mean these teapots are up to twenty-five per cent lighter than other cheaper but similar products. The Mayu teapot is also available as a special edition that features a handle coated with gold leaf.

Designer
Ken Okuyama

Source
Kikuchi Hojudo Inc.

Material(s)
Cast iron, enamel, aluminium alloy

Dimensions
Width: 14.5 cm
Depth: 10.8 cm
Height: 10 cm

Takayama Chasen tea whisk

Given the cultural importance of the Japanese tea ceremony, the origins of the Takayama Chasen tea whisk are steeped in history. According to legend, they were first made in the middle of the Muromachi period, covering the years 1336 to 1573, at the request of Murata Jukō, the founder of the simple tea ceremony, or *wabi-cha*. Evidence suggests that the emperor, Go-Tsuchimikado, was gifted tea whisks made by the craftsman Takayama Minbunojo Nyudo Sosetsu. They were originally known as Takaho Chasen but, for reasons that are unclear to this day, the name was later changed to Takayama Chasen.

Takayama Chasen tea whisks are fashioned from a bamboo tube with, typically, 128 thin bamboo slivers making up the whisk, which is bent and tied entirely by hand. The whisks are designed specifically to evenly mix the hot water and tea powder and are not particularly durable, sometimes lasting for just a single use. This follows the ethos of the tea ceremony, where each meeting is considered precious and can never be precisely repeated.

Designer
Takayama Minbunojo Nyudo Sosetsu

Source
ochaandco.com

Material
Bamboo

Dimensions
Diameter (approx.): 5 cm
Height (approx.): 10 cm

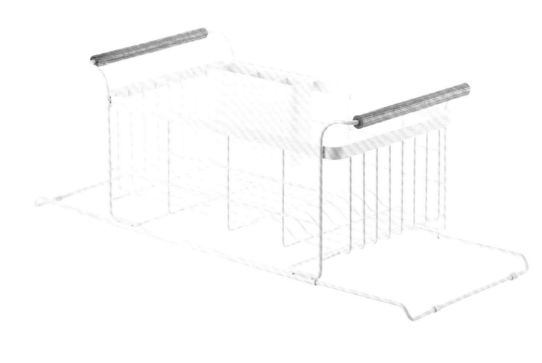

Tosca dish drainer

Products manufactured by the respected homeware design company Yamazaki make it into practically every room in the Japanese-styled home. Furniture for the hallway and the living room appears earlier in this book, and the kitchen is no exception.

The Yamazaki Tosca dish draining rack is a great example of yet another humdrum product that the Japanese design aesthetic has managed to elevate to something more attractive and desirable. The design of the metal rack itself, with its integral cutlery holder, is not revolutionary but, unlike many other drainers, the high sides help to prevent larger items toppling out. Wooden handles on either side provide a sense of quality, and the whole assembly sits neatly in a tray that incorporates a small tube which drains excess water directly into the sink. This neat device means the drainer can be used in smaller kitchens that do not have dedicated draining areas next to the sink.

Design
Yamazaki

Source
Yamazaki

Material(s)
Steel, wood, plastic

Dimensions
Width: 47 cm
Depth: 33.5 cm
Height: 20 cm

String strainer

The Japanese designer Taku Omura, founder of
the successful Tokyo-based studio oodesign, is an
architecture graduate who has designed a range
of homeware items alongside furniture and full
interiors. His best-known design, which won first
prize at the annual Kawasaki Industrial Design
Competition in 2011, is his string strainer. There are
countless strainer designs on the market, but this
one stands out because the 'strings' that form the
bulk of the strainer are very flexible and can be
pulled apart to dislodge items of food that get
stuck between them. This makes the strainer easier
to clean and therefore more hygienic.

The strainer is made from an interesting product
known as UNI-PELE. It is an eco-friendly resin
manufactured in Japan in two forms: TAK-REM,
which is a compound resin mixed with bamboo
powder; and BER-REM, which contains bran
powder. The material is fully biodegradable and can
withstand temperatures up to 120°C/250°F.

Designer
Taku Omura

Source
oodesign

Material
UNI-PELE eco-friendly resin

Dimensions
Diameter: 23 cm
Height: 10 cm

EATING

The dining room

A Japanese-style dining room shouldn't contain very much: it might even seem plain to Western eyes. But the intention behind Japanese design is not about impressing people; it's about making your home feel pleasing to them – and nowhere is that more relevant than the dining room. Besides which, there is beauty in simplicity: sparseness allows you to properly take in your surroundings, and paring things back to focus only on the essentials can feel surprisingly liberating.

Decide whether you want a traditional or contemporary feel, keep the furniture to a minimum, allow plenty of room around each piece so that the room feels spacious, and pick your accessories carefully: detail matters. Keeping the focus on a few, select pieces allows them to shine and your guests to fully appreciate them. The detail in Japanese accessories tends to be exquisite: handmade *washi* lanterns, glossy lacquered bowls, antique chests or delicately painted folding screens are just a few of your many options.

East versus West

The only essential items you need are a table (preferably wooden) and seating, so it makes sense to start there and build your room around them. If you want a traditional feel, it's best to go for a low-level table and floor seating, either *zabuton* or *zaisu* (floor chairs that have a back but no legs). If you'd rather have Western-style seating, there are plenty of options by Japanese designers to choose from. At the higher end, Conde House specializes in Japanese-influenced furniture: the dramatic Hakama table (see pages 132–3) would look stunning as the centrepiece of any dining-room. More affordably, Muji's range of dining room furniture offers clean lines and natural oak frames.

▲ Crockery should not be too perfect: look out for handmade, vintage or one-of-a-kind items that show the mark of their maker.

▶ If you want a Japanese-style dining room but dislike sitting on the floor, a horigotatsu *may be the solution: a recessed floor underneath means you can sit on* zabuton *but stretch out your legs as with Western-style seating. Some tables can also be slotted down into the floor to enable the room to be used for other purposes.*

▲ This full-length window brings nature into the dining room, while the latticed porch outside casts shadows across the table – a significant element in Japanese aesthetics.

▶ Exposed beams and columns add colour and texture to this large room, while low-hanging paper lanterns enhance the light from the large screened windows.

You can choose from chairs or benches, while a slightly lower table height adds to the understated Japanese feel. Keep your room layout asymmetrical: Japanese design reveres asymmetry and irregular balance for its dynamic beauty.

Lighting

If your table is low to the ground, keep your light sources similarly low. Use floor and table lamps rather than overhead lighting: paper shades or opaque lanterns will evoke the right tone and give your room a soft, warm glow. Shigeru Uchida's Paper Moon lamps offer simple forms and subtle illumination, while Isamu Noguchi's classic Akari lanterns were originally conceived as a way of sculpting with light.

If you have pendant lights and want to make the most of them, you can nod to tradition with simple paper shades (hang several in different shapes and sizes for contrast), or you could opt for more of a statement piece. Contemporary Japanese designers such as Toshiyuki Tani have found new ways to combine Western style with traditional Japanese elements to create new forms that still feel quintessentially Japanese. Tani's delicate yet dramatic Hokore bamboo pendant light (see pages 134–5) draws the eye and casts intricate shadows through its many layers.

Setting the table

Keep your dining-room table free of clutter: the way a table is laid is just as important as the food you serve. Ceramic or earthenware crockery in soft colours that complement the room work well in the Japanese-style dining room – think rounded edges, organic shapes and contrasting textures. *Wabi-sabi* is about finding beauty in the handmade and uneven, in objects that may be old or even broken but which have also been carefully mended. The goal is not a pristine arrangement but rather one that is perfectly imperfect. Items that show their maker's marks, that reveal the craftsmanship behind their creation, are revered above those that do not. Lacquered serving bowls, bamboo trays and wooden place mats are another way to introduce Japanese elements to your room, as are textiles: a table runner and napkins in contrasting but complementary colours and patterns will add beauty and texture to your table.

Tea space

Traditionally, Japanese homes often contained a space for tea drinking – either a separate building in the garden or a room or area inside dedicated to a tea ceremony (*chanoyu*). This highly ritualized tea ceremony was intended to purify and cleanse, and the principles of tea (harmony, respect, purity and tranquillity) were reflected in both the ceremony and the room in which it took place. In modern homes, such a space is less common, but by using natural materials (*tatami* mats or similar rush matting on the floor, or hardwood flooring), soft diffused lighting and muted colours, you can evoke a similar sense of tranquil contemplation in your dining room. If you want to serve tea, an iron kettle and handle-less bowls for drinking are traditional, or you could go for a more modern look with a minimalist classic like the Hakusan P-type tea service (see pages 126–7). Either way, presentation is just as important as taste when it comes to tea.

Case study

Designer/Owner Daniel Schoenen > **Year(s)** 2008 > **Place** Freiburg, Germany

The beauty of a traditional Japanese space for dining is that it is flexible: furniture can be moved and stored away easily, unlike more permanent Western-style dining tables and chairs, leaving the space to be used for other activities. This dining room can be used for eating or for a tea ceremony (*chanoyu*), or for something else altogether: the *tatami* mat flooring is comfortable to sit and walk on and can be used to mark out space for different activities.

Low tables and cushion seating work well in smaller spaces because they are unobtrusive: this table also has extendable leaves on different sides to create more room when needed. Another tip for small rooms is to choose furniture that lets light pass through, such as tables with legs rather than solid bases.

Avoid too much decoration on a dining table – the iron tea kettle here works well as a pop of colour against a neutral background. Generally you want food and dinnerware to be the main focus. As always, the overall feel of the room is simple and fuss-free, but that doesn't mean there is no adornment at all. Here, the chest, with its ornate front and carefully displayed accessories, and the artwork hanging above, function as a modern alternative to the traditional alcove (*tokonoma*).

Seating *A* zabuton *is a floor cushion designed for seating, and can also be used with a zaisu, a type of legless chair like the one that can be seen behind the table.*

Floor *A* tatami *mat floor is both traditional and practical. Unit or Oki tatami are suitable for Western rooms and can be placed directly on hard flooring. Be careful when using chairs though, as you run the risk of damaging the* tatami *mats.*

Lighting *If you're sitting on the floor, it makes sense to keep your sources of light lower to the ground rather than overhead. This minimalist bamboo and paper lamp or* andon *feels both traditional and modern in its simplicity.*

Art *The wall hanging provides the main focal point of the room, although its muted colour palette is not overbearing. Choosing artwork that is reminiscent of traditional motifs, such as the koi carp, is a subtle way to incorporate a sense of Japanese style.*

Storage *Antique Japanese chests* (tansu) *provide storage as well as being beautiful pieces of furniture in their own right, making them highly collectible. Low to the ground, this one sits well alongside the table and cushions.* Tansu *can be plain or patterned and adorned by ironwork or lacquer, and are made from various types of wood.*

Flower arrangement *Ikebana is the Japanese art of flower arrangement, a complex and disciplined art form that has evolved over hundreds of years. According to influential ikebana artist Toshiro Kawase, the ultimate intention is to expand your understanding of beauty and to see that 'the whole universe is contained within a single flower'.*

Signature colours

With a high-ceilinged room like this one, low-hanging pendant lights work well and are a good compromise between Western and Eastern lighting conventions: the different shapes and lengths give the arrangement a sculptural feel, and the asymmetric display provides the room with dynamic interest. The classic, simple paper shades hark back to traditional *andon* lighting, and when used filter the light to give a soft, diffused glow, as well as casting shadows across the space. In the daytime, large windows flood the room with natural light, with no curtains or blinds to get in the way or add fussiness. The unpainted wall between the window panes provides contrasting texture and colour, while the black frames ground the room.

The walls are shaded, with deeper colour lower down and lighter tones higher up, echoing the natural world. The colours used are warm and feel natural: pink isn't obviously connected with Japanese style, but here it draws out the earthiness and brown undertones of the furniture and exterior wall.

The polished hardwood floor contrasts subtly against the unvarnished furniture, while the patterned rug adds detail. The monochrome styling of the room, however, means there aren't any additional colours competing for attention.

The simple table and bench seating show the grain and texture of natural wood, the clean lines functional and understated. Earthenware crockery in tones that complement the walls complete the room, showing how important details are in Japanese design. Each item works in harmony with everything else.

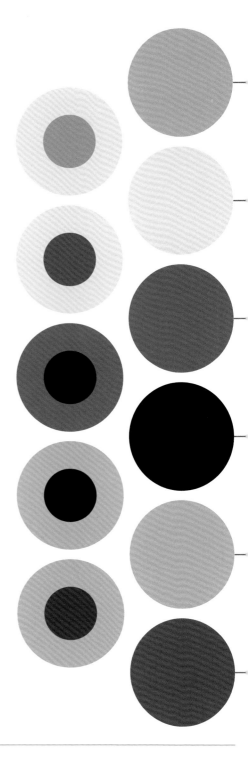

Hakusan P-type tea service

The well-known Japanese ceramics designer Masahiro Mori won a gold prize at Italy's Faenza International Ceramic Art Exhibition in 1975 with his design, created a year earlier, for the P-type tea service. No stranger to accolades, Mori won Japan's Good Design Award 110 times, and is famous for his G-type soy sauce bottle, which won the very first Good Design Award in 1960.

The distinctive handle of both the teacup and the coordinated teapot are 'P' shaped, thus supplying the product with its name. The square wooden saucer, which arguably provides the strongest element of Japanese flavour, is neatly chamfered and shaped to receive the cup, with an extra recess to accommodate the base of the handle. The otherwise minimalist design, with its refreshing blue and white colour scheme, helps to retain the product's modern look despite it being almost fifty years old.

Designer
Masahiro Mori

Source
Various retailers

Material(s)
Porcelain, wood

Dimensions
Teacup diameter: 6.5 cm
Teacup height: 7 cm
Saucer: 12 x 12 cm

YU dining chair

The furniture and homeware retailer MasterWal is one of the biggest in Japan, with branches in several major cities including Tokyo, Osaka and Yokohama (plus a US store in New York). The company prides itself on the high quality of its products, which are constructed from the best materials available, with wood (often walnut) appearing frequently.

The unique YU collection – *yu* means 'thoughtful' in Japanese – is arguably their most prestigious project to date. Mikiya Kobayashi was initially commissioned to create three chairs, but the collection has now expanded to include armchairs, sofas, tables and even a table tennis table with brass inlays and a leather net. The UC3 chair, with its elegant wooden frame, which features a subtle curve and a leather backrest, is the most iconic piece in the collection, and its form provides the basis for the visual aesthetic of the rest of the series.

Designer
Mikiya Kobayashi

Source
MasterWal

Material(s)
Walnut, leather

Dimensions
Width: 52 cm
Depth: 54 cm
Height: 79 cm

Donabe clay pot

One of the oldest styles of cooking pots used continuously in Japan for centuries, *donabe* translates as clay pot. These highly versatile pots, a kind of Japanese version of a Moroccan tagine, can be used to cook perfect rice as well as one-pot meals with numerous ingredients.

Originating from the Iga region, which is relatively close to the major urban centres of Kyoto and Osaka, the clay used to make *donabe* pots can withstand very high temperatures and so is ideal for cooking on a high heat. The clay is quite porous so heat builds up slowly, but efficient heat-retention properties mean the pots can keep food warm for longer and even continue to cook food for as long as twenty minutes after they're removed from a stove top or oven. Many typical Japanese kitchens will have at least one of these pots, which are used to serve meals as well as cook them.

Designer
Traditional

Source
Native and Co.

Material(s)
Clay

Dimensions
Diameter: 26 cm
Height: 21 cm

Hakama dining table

Despite its uniquely Japanese look, the Hakama dining table was designed as a commission for Conde House by the Hamburg-based partnership Maly Hoffmann Kahleyss (MHK). Much of the work of Peter Maly, Birgit Hoffmann and Christoph Kahleyss is clearly influenced by a Japanese design aesthetic and, like several other pieces in this book, the Hakama table was commissioned in response to the Fukushima nuclear disaster of 2011.

Hakama were the traditional style of wide trousers worn by samurai, the powerful military caste of warriors that existed in Japan between the 12th and 19th centuries, and the table takes its inspiration from this association. The message behind the bold design is one of 'pressing on in the face of adversity', and it is easy to visualize the stance of a fierce samurai when viewing this piece.

Design
Maly Hoffmann Kahleyss (MHK)

Source
Conde House

Material(s)
Japanese oak, walnut

Dimensions
Width: 240 / 210 / 180 cm
Depth: 100 cm
Height: 71 cm

Hokore bamboo pendant light

Bamboo is one of the materials that particularly characterizes Japanese style; it is used for furniture, fixtures and fittings and even as part of the structure in very traditional buildings. There are said to be no fewer than 1,250 known varieties of bamboo in the world and 626 of them can be found in Japan.

Japanese designer Toshiyuki Tani's Sen lighting collection is constructed entirely out of thin bamboo strips, known as *sensuji-zaiku*, using sophisticated and traditional Suruga latticework techniques. The concept is based on the forms of flowers at the moment of blooming, and the visual effect is full of energy. The collection includes two pedestal table lights and this pendant light, named the Hokore light, which works really well suspended above a dining area. The spreading pattern cast by the bamboo strips on the ceiling is quite beautiful.

Designer
Toshiyuki Tani

Source
kozaimodern.com

Material
Bamboo

Dimensions
Width: 47 cm
Depth: 47 cm
Height: 27.5 cm

CLEANSING

The bathroom

Japan's geology shaped the development of its bathing culture: it has thousands of natural hot springs, known as *onsen*, which have long been used as public baths. Therapeutic and relaxing, hot springs – and the bathing facilities and inns built around them – influenced the way private bathrooms were designed. The Japanese-style bathroom is not simply about cleansing, although hygiene is extremely important: it is also a space to linger in, to spend time relaxing and rejuvenating.

Separate areas

Traditionally, Japanese bathrooms have distinct areas for different functions; the toilet is always partitioned off in some way. Bathing is seen as a relaxing activity, rather than primarily a hygienic one, so in addition to the tub there is often a separate area for undressing and washing. A folding screen (*byōbu*) is a lovely way to cordon off an area while bringing an authentic touch of Japanese decor to your room. It is often impractical to partition an already small space, however, so it's worth considering other ways in which to convey a sense of distinction. Using mats or small rugs can help to mark out different areas, as does grouping accessories or towels in particular parts of the room. As always, keeping the room free of clutter will help to make full use of the space.

▲ Banish clutter from your bathroom by incorporating some storage: keeping cleansing products out of sight will make your bathroom feel more spacious and relaxing.

▶ Siting the bath next to a window gives you the opportunity to enjoy a soak with a view!

Bathing

The traditional Japanese bathtub (*ofuro*) makes bathing feel truly therapeutic: made of cedar wood, which gives off a lovely fragrance, it is deep enough for you to soak up to the neck. You should already have cleaned yourself before entering the tub: its purpose is indulgence rather than hygiene. A free-standing, deep, Western-style bath conveys a similar sense of relaxation if an *ofuro* is not

practical for your bathroom, or you could create the effect of one by using wooden bath panels to conceal an acrylic bath. You could also employ certain accessories to create a calm, soothing environment: a wooden bath rack, marble soap dish or a traditional Japanese bath bucket made from cypress wood are all useful items that will bring a touch of nature into the room. Keep cleansing products stored away rather than letting them stack up around the bath, and use lanterns or candles at night for mood lighting and to create shadows to enhance the experience.

Room with a view

In Japanese houses, what is outside is an important consideration: gardens are often designed with an eye to how they will look when viewed from inside. This is also important in a bathroom, so windows should be low enough to enjoy the view from your bathtub, bringing daylight and greenery in and unifying the outside world with the bathroom. If that's not possible, or if privacy is a concern, a reed or bamboo blind or a *shōji* screen over the window will still allow the light through. If you don't have a window, you could use a *shōji* panel to hide away shelves for storage. They also work very well as sliding pocket doors, which can be an effective way to maximize space if your room is small.

◄ A bath stool and bucket are classically Japanese bathroom accessories, and especially useful in wet rooms or larger shower enclosures. Sitting down and ladling water over yourself is a relaxing experience – and more eco-friendly than a conventional shower.

Natural materials

Where possible, take your colour cues from nature: a wooden bath, floor or wall panel will give your bathroom texture and warmth. The rivulets, veins and varying textures of stone can be displayed to stunning effect in a bathroom: slate, marble or granite are wonderful, if expensive, natural stone options for walls and floors (make sure floor tiles are slip-resistant) as long as they are sealed and cleaned properly. Stone-effect porcelain tiles can also be remarkably effective and are much cheaper and easier to maintain. Pebble or river rock floors use small round stones and are another way to bring nature into your room (though bear in mind they use a lot of grout, which can be tricky to keep clean). Concrete is also a great choice for

bathrooms (it generally deals well with humidity), and has been widely used in Japanese architecture: whether smoothed or textured, it can look just as stunning as wood or stone.

Beyond the materials themselves, there are no hard-and-fast rules on colour schemes: instead focus on the dual purpose of the Japanese-style bathroom (to cleanse and to relax) and consider what works best for you. Do you want your bathroom to feel clean and uplifting? If so, go for white or pale tiled walls, neutral floors and as much natural light as possible (mirrors will help to maximize the daylight available). If cosiness is more important, darker tones will set the right mood. In both cases, indoor plants will provide colour and that all-important link to the outside world.

Case study

Designer/Owner Meryl Santopietro > **Year(s)** 2009 > **Place** Rhode Island, USA

As much a place for relaxation as for cleansing, the Japanese bathroom is somewhere you want to linger. This room hits all the right notes in providing a serene atmosphere, at one with nature. A lot of thought has gone into every detail to make it feel very special.

Window position matters in a Japanese bathroom – if possible, you should be able to enjoy the view from the bathtub. Here, the raised picture windows wrap around the room, flooding the space with light and drawing the outside world in without compromising privacy. The plants inside harmonize perfectly with the trees visible through the windows, creating a real sense of a natural sanctuary.

Ideally, every bathroom should have a deep soaking tub (*ofuro*) in which you can immerse yourself up to the neck. It's not intended for hygiene purposes; it's about relaxing the body and mind. Traditionally, such tubs are made from fragrant cedar, though there are other options available today such as tiles or fibreglass. This one is made from honey-toned cast concrete: it coordinates perfectly with the rest of the room and will only improve with age as its patina develops.

The range of materials used – wood, stone, concrete, glass and tile – creates a warm colour palette in harmonious tones, adding depth as well as providing subtle textural contrast. The bamboo towel rack is a nice touch and brings another natural element to the room.

Light *Plenty of natural light makes this room bright and airy. If your bathroom doesn't get much or any daylight, use mirrors to reflect light and imitate the feel of a window.*

Alcove *Recessed niches or shelves give you extra space that can be used to display objects such as candles, plants or ornaments.*

Towels *Carefully chosen to complement the room's colour scheme, nothing detracts from the feeling of peace and tranquillity engendered here.*

Storage *This wicker chest is a beautiful and unusual way to keep cleaning products out of sight when not in use.*

Shells *This simple but effective arrangement of shells in a glass vase is a great way to bring a bit of nature into your bathroom. A selection of stones of varying colours and textures would also work well.*

Shower screen *Japanese bathrooms tend to have separate areas for different functions. The glass screen encloses a separate shower area, intended for cleansing before entering the bathtub.*

Signature colours

At first glance there doesn't seem to be much to this bathroom, but, as is often the case with Japanese interiors, paying close attention yields rewards. Here the colour palette is drawn from the materials themselves, raw and unadorned.

This is the area of a bathroom where one cleanses with the shower before moving to the tub to relax: despite its functional purpose, aesthetics are not overlooked. It is an exercise in simplicity and textural contrasts. The natural variation of the wood-panelled wall offers a subtly rich array of shades, and the lack of decoration means the texture, grain and knotty imperfections can be clearly seen and appreciated. The lighter wood of the bath stool and bucket and the bleached wooden slats of the draining area stand out against the darker-hued wall, while the cool blue-grey tones of the stone offset the warmer wood. In a bathroom, both materials will change over time as water adds a patina and dulls their colours but, as the concept of *wabi-sabi* shows us, that only makes it a more attractive space.

The copper-ringed bath bucket is traditionally used to rinse the body after washing or simply to wash your face, though it can also be used as a caddy for soap or shampoo. Japanese cypress has a fresh scent and is naturally resistant to mould and mildew, making it a great choice for bathroom accessories. The gleam of the bucket's copper bands is balanced against the chrome shower bar, the modern fixture contrasting effectively with the traditional bucket and bath stool.

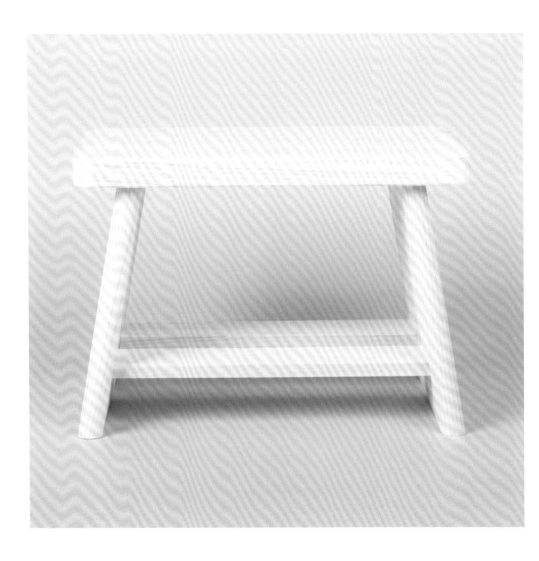

Hinoki bath stool

Hinoki is a species of cypress native to central Japan and is renowned for its high quality as a construction timber and for use in the furniture industry. It is used extensively in the building of temples and shrines, and for the manufacture of traditional wooden baths and *masu* rice boxes. The wood carries a distinctive lemon scent and is highly resistant to rot and mould.

In Japanese homes, showers are often taken seated; it is seen as a more relaxing way to unwind while bathing. To facilitate this, classic Hinoki bath stools come in many varied but similar forms and are generally sized to provide a comfortable seating position for an average-sized adult – and of course to fit in a tub or shower cubicle. Given its excellent water-resistant properties, Hinoki wood is the perfect material to make stools that are used in a wet environment, be it the bathroom or in a sauna.

Designer
Traditional

Source
Native & Co.

Material
Hinoki wood (Japanese cypress)

Approximate dimensions
Width: 30 cm
Depth: 18 cm
Height: 23 cm

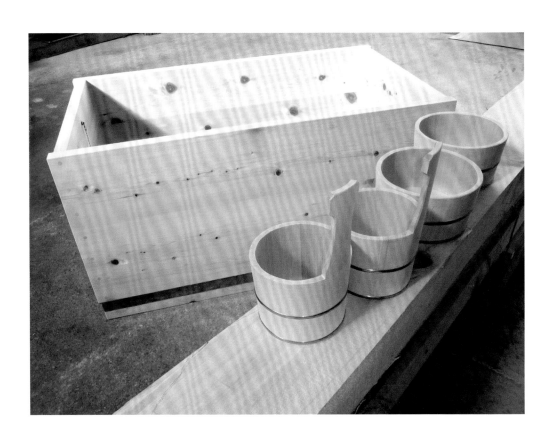

Hinoki bath

The water-resistant properties of Hinoki, or Japanese cypress, are discussed on the previous spread (see pages 148–9), so it comes as no surprise that it is used extensively in the manufacture of traditional wooden bathtubs. Nothing symbolizes the style of a Japanese bathroom more than a wooden tub, and a long daily soak in warm water is something of a ritual for many Japanese people. This goes beyond basic hygiene and is seen very much as a health benefit that stimulates blood circulation and helps to prevent everyday ailments such as colds and influenza.

Hinoki bath tubs are made in many different shapes and sizes, and are built for outdoor as well as indoor use. They can be high- or shallow-sided, they can be raised on a platform or set into the floor, and are typically straight-sided; sloped sides, if they appear, are usually angled quite steeply when compared to a Western-style bath tub. Circular tubs, or longer tubs with rounded ends, are also popular.

Designer
Iacopo Torrini

Source
bartokdesign.com

Material
Hinoki wood (Japanese cypress)

Dimensions
Various

Pond candle holder

Candlelight enhances the relaxing atmosphere of a welcoming bathroom the world over. Ornamenting the surround of a bath tub with an array of candles so the flames are reflected in the water can create a very soothing effect.

The wonderfully minimal Pond candle holder, designed by Daisuke Kitagawa, goes one step further. The round form holds a single tea light, and its highly polished finish reflects and expands the warm glow of the candle's flame from the encompassing bowl. The surrounding space is in turn reflected and distorted in the bowl, creating a pleasing visual effect. The Pond holder shouldn't be restricted to the bathroom as it is well suited for use in any room of the house. An elongated unit, which holds three tea lights in row, is particularly apt for use as tableware.

Designer
Daisuke Kitagawa

Source
Daisuke Kitagawa Design

Material
Aluminium

Dimensions
Height: 3.8 cm
Diameter: 10.2 cm

Toto washlet toilet

The sanitaryware manufacturer Tokyo Toki Co. Ltd, later renamed TOTO, was established in 1917 by Kazuchika Okura. Ironically, given the importance placed on Japanese bathroom culture today, toilet facilities were surprisingly unsophisticated at that time, and Okura wanted to develop similar sanitary ceramics to those commonly used in Europe and America.

Fast-forward to 1980, and TOTO launched the Washlet, a revolutionary new design featuring an integrated bidet system that would quickly become both a cultural and commercial sensation. The current range of Washlets feature warm-water cleansing systems, heated seats, air purification systems and even remote controls. This is bathroom hygiene taken to a new level. All models in the range are quite compact so can be easily fitted in smaller bathrooms and they are also wall-mounted, making it a simple task to clean underneath the unit.

Designer
TOTO

Source
TOTO

Material
Urea resin

Dimensions (Washlet RX)
Width: 38.3 cm
Depth: 57.9 cm
Height: 14.6 cm

Imabari towel

Imabari towels are so-called because they originate from Imabari, a city in Ehime prefecture. The city is home to a large cotton-processing industry with an emphasis on towel manufacturing; around sixty per cent of all towels made in Japan come from the area. Towels made from Imabari cotton are ranked among the finest-quality towels in the world due to the superior softness and absorbability of the fabric. These qualities are said to be a result of the naturally soft local water that is used in the towel-making process.

After more than 100 years of local production, the towel-making industry in Imabari suffered from the increasing availability of cheap foreign alternatives, but the region's manufacturers pulled together to focus on the unique quality of their materials, and they are now enjoying a resurgence.

Designer
Traditional

Source
Imabari Towel Japan

Material
Cotton

Dimensions

Face towel
Width: 34 cm
Length: 35 cm

Hand towel
Width: 34 cm
Length: 80 cm

Bath towel
Width: 65 cm
Length: 120 cm

RESTING

The bedroom

We all know how vital rest is, and given we spend a good third of our lives in bed, it's important that the bedroom is somewhere that feels relaxing and soothing. But whereas in the West a bedroom typically contains heavy, inflexible furniture, making it unsuitable for any other function, in the Japanese tradition the bedroom is seen as just another fluidly delineated space. Evaluating your bedroom with this in mind will help you to keep furniture and possessions to a minimum and maximize the space you have to good effect: beyond a bed and somewhere to store your clothes, what else do you really need? Keeping your bedroom as open as possible will go a long way towards making it a calming and relaxed space. Combine that with a sense of nature and a light or subdued colour scheme and you have the perfect recipe for a good night's sleep.

Sleeping

Portable furniture and space-saving storage solutions are Japanese specialities, and Japanese ingenuity when it comes to stacking or folding can be seen in its traditions: think about *origami* or *byōbu* (see page 32). Even bedding is intended to be portable – the traditional futon was designed to be folded or rolled up and put away during the day. These days that may be less common (though many will still hang out futons to air regularly), but the futon retains its usefulness as a flexible piece of furniture, used as both bed and sofa. If the idea of sleeping on *tatami* mats doesn't appeal, you could raise your futon up on a slatted platform base or substitute it for a mattress: the main aim is to keep your furniture low to the ground and have plenty of space around each piece to engender a sense of balance, stability and openness.

▲ *The carved wooden screen over the headboard mimics traditional* shōji *screen panelling. The bed is on a raised section, under which storage drawers are placed.*

▸ *A Western-style mattress on* tatami *mat flooring may be more comfortable than a futon for some, while still adhering to the conventions of Japanese style.*

▲ Diffused natural light and plenty of space around the bed makes this room feel calm and conducive to relaxation.

▶ Natural linen and cotton fabrics are used on this traditional platform bed. The large plant placed in the corner works in harmony with the natural wood bed frame.

Storage

Once you've streamlined the contents of your bedroom, you need somewhere to put everything. Traditionally, many Japanese homes made use of a *kaidan dansu* in the bedroom – a stepped chest containing drawers for storing prized possessions. For a modern take on this classic piece of furniture, try Keiji Ashizawa's Sutoa storage chest for Frama, with its simple, clean lines and beautiful oak

drawers. It's even portable, like the original *tansu* chests, so can be moved around easily.

Textiles and lighting

Stick to organic fabrics in your bedroom, such as cotton, silk and linen. Light, neutral shades or unbleached material will give your room a natural and soothing feel, although dark blue or indigo can also work within a Japanese-influenced scheme if you want deeper tones for contrast. Hardwood floors with rush mats for warmth underfoot are more typical of Japanese style than carpet and will add natural colour and contrasting texture. Opaque screens over your windows will give you a more traditional feel, keeping your room light but private; window blinds in a neutral colour are an easy modern alternative and will give you the same result. If you have curtains, choose translucent fabric and keep them open as much as possible to allow the light in. Artificial lighting should be soft and diffused, and low to the ground to match the furniture. If you have overhead lighting, choose a pendant fixture that works with a suspended cable or flex so you can hang it low.

Decoration through detail

Japanese-style rooms should feel natural and comfortable, not overly stylized or designed, and the bedroom is no exception. Keeping the broader canvas of the room plain and simple allows you to pay attention to the detail, which is where you can bring in a more decorative touch. If everything else is neutral, adding a patterned bedspread or embroidered cushion to your bed will draw the eye without overbearing the senses. A free-standing *shōji* or decorative *byōbu* screen made with

translucent paper, opaque glass or silk panels will add intricate detail and can be used to conceal a pile of messy clothes or provide privacy. The aim is to create a sense of mindful attention to detail, a room where every item has its place and has been added with careful intention.

Plants

It has been said before but it bears repeating: living in harmony with nature is a hugely important component of Japanese style. You can bring the natural world into your bedroom in a number of ways to give a sense of freshness and peace to the space. Use natural, raw materials such as wood, bamboo and cotton; choose artwork depicting landscapes, birds, animals or florals to decorate a wall; add house plants for greenery; or make your own sculptural arrangement from a piece of driftwood.

Case study

Designer/Owner Scott-lee > **Year(s)** 2009 > **Place** Seoul, Korea

This soothing bedroom is an excellent example of how to combine Western and Eastern influences effectively: the custom-made low-slatted platform is a clever compromise between a bedframe and a *tatami* mat. Here the platform also functions as a kind of *tokonoma*, displaying a small shrine.

In keeping with the Japanese principle of *ma*, or negative space, the room is minimally furnished, clean and uncluttered with plenty of room around the bed. The futon can be stored away when not needed so that the platform can be flexibly used, perhaps switching to seating in the daytime. The paper lamps provide low floor lighting, characteristic of traditional Japanese *andon*, while daylight is filtered through the floor-length opaque glass panels (which also provide privacy), in a nod to traditional *shōji* screens.

Notice there is little in the way of decoration – the bedroom should be a place to relax and rest, and keeping the space free of distraction and clutter helps to achieve that. The colour scheme is classically Japanese, reflecting warm natural hues in the wood floor and platform, while the bed linen offers complementary tones of brown and white. The pattern draws the eye and provides interesting contrast, without dominating the room. The slatted platform also provides a subtle but effective contrast in texture against the sanded boards and the smooth glass panels.

Greenery *Plants add colour and bring nature into the room – an essential requirement in Japanese homes. An umbrella plant is a great choice for a houseplant as you can't over-water it – its roots need to stay as wet as possible.*

Multi-purpose furniture *The extended platform bedframe avoids the need for bedside tables, thus keeping the room streamlined and easily adaptable for other uses.*

Bed *Futons are quintessentially Japanese and are sufficiently pliable to be moved and stored easily. Setting your futon up on a slatted base like this one avoids the need for regular airing, however, which is otherwise essential.*

Ariake andon *Traditional bedside lamps in Japan are small enough to sit beside your pillow. They are made from paper shades stretched over bamboo, wooden or metal frames. Originally the andon was hand-held and contained oil for burning: the paper protected the flame from the wind.*

Signature colours

Although a colour palette based on pale shades and natural materials makes for a classic Japanese-style bedroom, it's perfectly possible to introduce other colours successfully, as can be seen here. This calm, inviting space is a great example of how to mix traditional and contemporary elements to stunning effect.

Using the same shade to cover the walls and ceiling is a clever way to make a room feel larger by creating an endless plane of colour: this mid-tone blue is a soothing choice and is subtly echoed in the smaller glass vase, which glows against the window. The strips of wood used to partition the wall and ceiling echo the horizontal and vertical lines of the *shōji* screens in front of the window and the *tatami* mats on the floor, unifying the space.

A stronger colour scheme also allows for more dramatic bed linen: this luxurious deep teal fabric is set off well against the lighter walls, and its floral pattern feels delicate and reminiscent of cherry blossom, that significant Japanese emblem. The pink and white flowers are matched by the sprays of real blossom in the vases, bringing an all-important touch of nature inside.

The low tables, paper light shade and platform bed honour the conventions of classic Japanese style, while the *tatami* mats and *shōji* screens provide natural warm colour and another connection to traditional design. The sliding screens keep the lighting soft and ensure privacy while also allowing for the outside world to be brought into the room as desired, making a real feature of the window and its views.

Futon bed

The popularity of the futon bed has grown significantly outside Japan in the past few decades. Owners of flats and bedsits the world over enjoy its wonderfully practical benefits, namely that it can be folded back during the day to create extra space. People in the West are likely to recognize the wooden-pallet style of futon that mimics a sofa bed, but in Japan traditional futons are more likely to consist of a padded mattress (*shikibuton*), a quilt (*kakebuton*), and a pillow (*makura*). The mattress is often set atop a *tatami* mat as an alternative to placing it directly on the floor, and the whole assembly can be rolled up and stored to one side when not in use.

The obtainability of a genuine futon will depend somewhat on your location and the availability of authentic Japanese futons from a local retailer. A visit to the website of a company such as Kyoto Nishikawa, a manufacturer with over 450 years of history, will help inform your choice.

Designer
Preben Christensen

Source
karup.eu

Material(s)
Principally cotton, plus hemp, wool, feathers, man-made fibre

Dimensions
Various

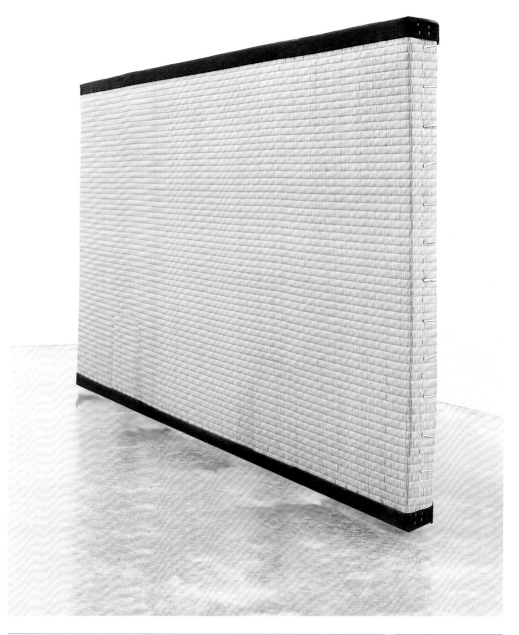

Tatami mat

The word *tatami* is derived from the verb *tatamu*, which means 'to fold' or 'to pile'. *Tatami* mats, historically a luxury item that only the wealthy could afford, have now become synonymous with Japanese style. Prior to the end of the 17th century, the floors of commoners' homes would have been packed earth with a covering of rushes, but gradually *tatami* mats became more affordable. Today, it is rare to find entire homes with *tatami* floor coverings, but it is common to find one or two mats in a bedroom, especially if used with a futon (see pages 170–1).

Mats are always made with an aspect ratio of 2:1, where the length is exactly twice that of the width. Standard sizes differ from region to region; in Kyoto, *tatami* generally measure 0.995 by 1.91 metres and are known as *Kyōma tatami*; in Nagoya, they are 0.91 by 1.82 metres and are called *Ainoma tatami*; while in Tokyo they are 0.88 by 1.76 metres and are referred to as *Edoma* or *Kantōma tatami*. Traditionally, the dimensions of rooms in Japanese houses were dictated by the dimensions of grouped *tatami* mats covering the total floor area.

Designer
Preben Christensen

Source
karup.eu

Material(s)
Rice straw, compressed wood chip, rush straw, various fabrics for edging

Dimensions
Various, but always in a 2:1 ratio.

Artemide reading light

Naoto Fukasawa has enjoyed an international
career, working in the United States from 1989
until a move back to Tokyo in 1996 while working
for the renowned design firm IDEO. He established
Naoto Fukasawa Design in 2003 and has since
created products for many leading brands
including Artemide, the Milan-based manufacturer
of high-end lighting products.

The specially commissioned Artemide
Demetra range includes a number of wall-mounted
spotlights as well as the exceedingly stylish AR
reading lamps, which can be purchased in both
table, wall-mounted and floor-standing options.
Finishes include white, black and anthracite grey
options. The dimmable LED light source set into
the disc-like body of the light casts a warm white
glow, ideal for reading, and the entire range carries
a very green A++ energy rating when combined
with the correctly rated bulb.

Designer
Naoto Fukasawa

Source
Artemide

Material(s)
Aluminium, technopolymer

Dimensions
Width: 63.5 cm
Length: 130 cm
Height: 63.7 cm

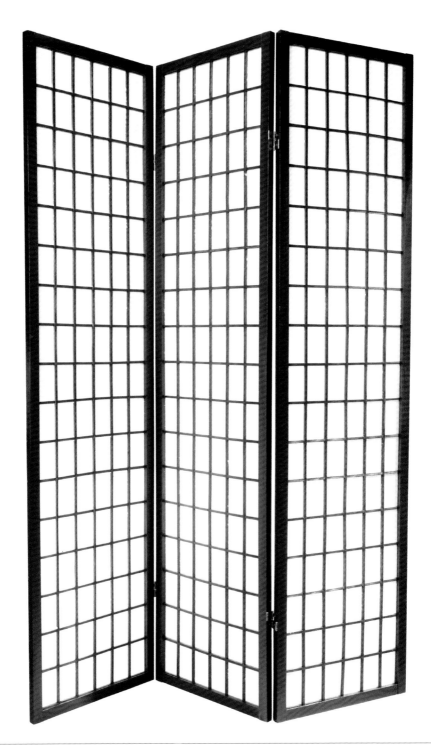

Shōji screen

Traditional Japanese architecture is probably characterized most strikingly by *shōji*, a door, window, or room divider constructed with translucent paper (*washi* paper, which is made from bark fibres) stretched across a wooden frame that borders a lattice of either wood or bamboo strips. Modern *shōji* can also be made using plastic as an alternative to wood, and the *washi* paper element can be replaced by modern materials, although it is worth noting that *washi* is more durable than paper made from wood pulp. *Shōji* is never used for exterior surfaces; if utilized as a door or window it always sits inside a sliding glass screen.

Shōji screens are great for dividing rooms and for providing some privacy in the dressing area of a bedroom. They are constructed using a hinged concertina design, which makes it easy to fold them away when they are not in use, and the design also means they are free-standing. There is no traditional limit to the number of separate panels that can be included; screens usually incorporate between three and six panels.

Designer
Gabriel Tan

Source
ariakecollection.com

Material(s)
Wood/bamboo, *washi* paper

Dimensions
Width: 171 cm
Depth: 70 cm
Height: 165 cm

Sutoa storage chest

Keiji Ashizawa's profile as a designer was raised in 2011 following his work with the Ishinomaki Laboratory (see pages 54–5). Earlier in his career, Ashizawa worked as both an architect and a steel fabricator, and this combination of skills has strongly influenced his approach to his interior design projects and the furnishings within them.

The Danish furniture manufacturer Frama, located in central Copenhagen, works closely with commissioned architects and designers across all of their ranges of furniture and interior fittings. Ashizawa's Sutoa storage chest (*sutoa* translates as 'store' or 'contain') is a wonderfully aesthetic take on a traditional chest of drawers. A delicate steel frame of runners that incrementally decrease in size holds a series of seven walnut boxes, with a discreet gap where the front of each box overlaps the box below it. These gaps act as the 'handles', allowing each box to be opened in the manner of a standard drawer. Two small wheels at the back of the frame allow the chest to be repositioned easily for access or cleaning.

Designer
Keiji Ashizawa

Source
Frama

Material(s)
Walnut, steel

Dimensions
Width: 67 cm
Depth: 53 cm
Height: 116.5 cm

Caramella headboard

Hirashima, a furniture manufacturer based in
Yanagawa City, is known for its simple but clever
pieces that attempt to solve the day-to-day
problems experienced by many Japanese people
– living comfortably with limited space. The
solutions combine tables with bookshelves, convert
sofas into dining tables, and turn a bed and
headboard into a small office space with a desk.

The home office/bed, part of Hirashima's
Caramella range, certainly helps to support the
Japanese reputation for hard work and long hours.
A built-in bedside table can be swung sideways to
form a lap desk if you wish to work while sitting in
the bed itself, but the headboard is arguably more
interesting. A full-width desk topped with a narrow
but functional shelf is built onto the back of the
headboard. There is also a drawer with four
compartments that sits beneath the desk, and
a separate filing cabinet-style unit that can be
positioned as the user wishes. A selection of
bed widths are available, ranging from a narrow
126 cm to a kingsize 231 cm.

Designer
Nobuo Mori

Source
Hirashima Inc.

Material
Walnut

Dimensions
Width: 126/231 cm
Depth: 267 cm
Height: 91 cm

Prism wardrobe

This has to be the wardrobe of choice for anyone
that takes great pride in showing off their clothing
collection. Designed by Tokujin Yoshioka for the
renowned Italian glass furniture manufacturer Glas
Italia, the Prism wardrobe is made from 12 mm
tempered and thermo-welded glass with a polished
steel hanging bar. The doors are made of a slightly
lighter 8 mm glass and are opened and closed with
a precise push/pull system – the catch is released
when the door's surface is pushed gently inwards.
All joins are bevelled along the edges to reflect and
refract ambient light and a small glass shelf above
the mirrored base of the unit is provided for storing
shoes or accessories.

The piece is unashamedly contemporary and,
although not obviously Japanese in style, the
ethos behind the design is sound. It is a simple
and functional object with no significant
embellishments, from a designer that has
mastered the art of transparency.

Designer
Tokujin Yoshioka

Source
Glas Italia

Material(s)
Tempered glass, steel

Dimensions
Width: 100 cm
Depth: 60 cm
Height: 195 cm

Ripple vase

The successful Tokyo-based studio oodesign
was founded in 2009 by the Japanese designer
Taku Omura (see also pages 112–13) and
specializes principally in the design of functional
homeware pieces as well as the design of furniture
and full interiors. With this in mind, the Ripple
vase is something of a departure; its function
is simply to look beautiful instead of having a
task-based functionality.

The Ripple is not a vase in the conventional
sense, but rather a small disc that is designed to
float on any area of water—whether it be a vase or
a glass—with a hole in the centre to hold a single
stem. The disc is made from clear polycarbonate
and shaped to look like the radiating ripple effect
one sees when an object is dropped into still water.
Once the user has mastered the trick of balancing
the stem perfectly in the centre of the vase, it can
be floated in a larger container filled with water.
The effect is entirely convincing.

Designer
Taku Omura / oodesign

Source
stylestore.com

Material
Polycarbonate

Dimensions
Diameter: 5.2 cm
Height: 2 cm

Further resources

Books:

Koji Yagi. *A Japanese Touch for Your Home*. Kodansha: 1982

Penny Sparke. *Japanese Design*. Michael Joseph: 1987

Geeta Mehta, Kimie Tada and Noboru Murata. *Japan Style: Architecture + Interiors + Design*. Tuttle Publishing: 2005

Sunamita Lim. *Japanese Style: Designing with Nature's Beauty*. Gibbs Smith: 2007

Alexandra Black and Noboru Murata. *The Japanese House: Architecture and Interiors*. Scriptum Editions: 2000

Lisa Parramore, Chadine Flood Gong and Noboru Murata. *Japan Home: Inspirational Design Ideas*. Tuttle Publishing: 2009

Gian Carlo Calza. *Japan Style*. Phaidon: 2007

Rossella Menegazzo, Stefania Piotti. *WA: The Essence of Japanese Design*. Phaidon: 2014

Andrew Juniper. *Wabi Sabi: The Japanese Art of Impermanence*. Tuttle Publishing: 2003

Sarah Lonsdale. *Japanese Style*. Carlton Books: 2001

Patricia J. Graham. *Japanese Design: Art, Aesthetics & Culture*. Tuttle Publishing: 2014

Sîan Evans. *Contemporary Japanese Design*. Collins & Brown: 1991

Yoko Kawaguchi. *Serene Gardens: creating Japanese design and detail in the western garden*. New Holland: 2000

Matthias Dietz, Michael Mönninger. *Japanese Design*. Taschen: 1994

David N. Buck. *Responding to Chaos: Tradition, Technology, Society and Order in Japanese Design*. Spon Press: 2000

Gregory Irvine (ed). *Japanese Art and Design*. V&A Publishing: 2016

Websites:

Japan House (Japanese cultural centre, including exhibitions, shops, events and restaurants)
www.japanhouselondon.uk

Architonic (for information about design and architecture and designer biographies)
www.architonic.com

Wagumi
www.wagumi-j.com

The Japanese Shop
www.thejapaneseshop.co.uk

Japan Craft
www.japancraft.co.uk

Brandt Oriental Antiques
www.brandtasianart.com
(furniture, ceramics, art and embroidery)

Grays Antique Market
www.graysantiques.com

Credits

7, 8-9: Pixabay

10, 29, 169: Ahlens, www.ahlens.se

11T, 27, 38T, 38B, 47: Muuto, www.muuto.com

11B, 12, 13, 68, 116: Living4Media/
Matteo Manduzio

14, 18, 76, 80, 86, 132: Conde House, 2 Henry
Adams St., Showroom 152 San Francisco CA94103

15, 24-5, 26, 42-3, 93: Sinato, Tokyo. Project:
Fujigaoka M, photos by Toshiyuki Yano;
www.sinato.jp

16: Mitch Iburg Ceramics, www.mitchiburg.com

17, 114-5: Shutterstock/Photgraphee.eu

19: Yoshihara Woodworks

20T: 119, Kengo Kuma & Associates, KKAA.co.jp,

20B: Shutterstock/Hayk_Shalunts

21: www.nishizawaarchitects.com

23: Skandium www.skandium.com

28, 31T: Hotel Kabuki/Markzeff

30: BongGrit, flickr.com/photos/bonguri

31TR: Shutterstock/Hans Siegers

31B: Getty Images/Christian Kaden,
Satori-Nihon.de

32: Shutterstock/TokyoVideoStock

33T: Alamy/Bombay Black

33B: Shutterstock/Mark Schwettmann

34: Studio Sarah Wilmer, Architecture/Photo by
Ken Gutmaker Photography; www.studio-sw.com

35T: Living4Media/View Pictures; Architect: Foster
and Partners

35B, 114-15: © Jeremie Souteyrat

36: Alamy/Rich Iwasaki

37T: Getty Images/Owen Lin

37B: Shutterstock/Darunee Sakulsri

39T: Getty Images/R Creation

40-1, 69, 90-1: KAD Architectural Design;
www.k-a-d.jp

44: Getty Images/imagenavi

45: Getty Images/imagewerks Japan

46: Living4Media/Anderson Karl

48-51: Mata Design Studio, Project: Claremont
Residence; www.matadesign.com.au

53: Mind The Gap www.designvintage.co.uk/
collections/mind-the-gap

54: Ishinomaki Laboratory
www.ishinomaki-lab.org/about/

56: IKEA

58, 78: Nendo, www.nendo.jp/en

60, 62, 84, 110: Wayfair.co.uk

64-5: Getty Images/B&M Noskowski

66: Ariake/Sebastian Stadler,
www.ariakecollection.com

67: Simon Upton/The Interior Archive

70-3: Gap Interiors/House and Leisure/R. Smith

75: Natural Bed Company

82: hermanmiller.co.uk

88: B&B Italia

92: www.wijzijnkees.nl

94: Getty Images/Taiyou Nomachi

95: Studio Sarah Willmer, Architecture/Photo by
Jasper Sanidad; www.studio-sw.com

96-9: Alamy/Andreas von Einsiedel

101: www.wrenkitchens.com

102: Kamenoko Tawashi Nishio Shoten

104: Tokyobike, 87-9 Tabernacle Street, London EC2A 4BA

106: Kikuchi Hojudo, Inc.

108: Ocha & Co., 9-6 A Nishimachi Higashikawa, Hokkaido Japan 071-1425 ochaandco.com

112, 184: Taku Omura Oodesign oodesign.com

117: Getty Images/Sam+Yvonne

118: Alamy/John Esperanza

120-3: Alamy/Panther Media GmbH

125: Habitat UK Ltd.

126: CIBI 45 Keele Street, Collingwood VIC 3066 Melbourne Australia cibi.com.au

128: MasterWal www.masterwal.jp

130, 148: Native & Co. London www.nativeandco.com

134: Kozai Modern www.kozaimodern.com

136-7: Volkshotel by Hanna Maring, photo by Mark Groenveld; www.volkshotel.nl

138: Getty Images/MIXA

139: Getty Images/Ivan

140: www.espressodesign.co.uk

141, 161: Gap Interiors/Costas Picadas

142-5: Nat Rea/The Interior Archive

147: Getty Images/Iain Masterton

150: Bartok Design

152: Daisuke Kitagawa Design/ /Design For Industry Inc., photo by Hisashi Kudo

154: TOTO Courtesy of Industry Publicity Unit

156: Shikoku Tours

158 9, 170, 172: Karup Partners A/S, Denmark www.stylehouse.no

160: Shutterstock/Atiketta Sangasaeng

162: Getty Images/Junshi Nakamichi

163: Shutterstock / Scott-lee

164-7: Getty Images/Michael Boys/Corbis/VCG

174: Artemide www.artemide.com

176: Ariake www.ariakecollection.com

178: Frama www.framacph.com

180: Hirashima Inc. www.hirashima.petit.cc

182: Chaplins Luxury Furniture

184: The Japanese Design Shop

Every effort has been made to trace copyright holders to obtain their permission for the use of copyright material. The publisher apologizes for any errors or omissions in the aforementioned list and would be grateful if notified of any corrections that should be incorporated in future reprints or editions of this book.

Index

Author biographies

Olivia Bays is a writer and editor of adult non-fiction, and has worked on design and craft titles for HarperCollins, Virgin and Wiley, among other publishers. She fell in love with Japanese interior design after spending time in Japan in 2016, and subsequently started to research Japanese-inspired furniture and accessories. She lives in Cambridge, England, with her husband and two young sons, and dreams of minimalist living spaces.

Tony Seddon is a graphic designer and writer with over twenty-five years of publishing industry experience. He has written and designed numerous books including *Greetings from Retro Design* and *Let's Talk Type*, both published by Thames & Hudson. He lives in East Sussex, England with his wife and their beloved lurchers.

Cathelijne Nuijsink graduated in Architecture from Delft University of Technology, The Netherlands and The University of Tokyo, Japan before embarking on a PhD in East Asian Languages & Civilizations at the University of Pennsylvania, USA (MA, 2013. PhD, 2017). In her PhD thesis, she investigated the recent history of the single-family house in Japan as a product of intense theoretical examination and architectural experimentation. Currently, Nuijsink is a postdoc researcher at the Institute for the History and Theory of Architecture (gta) at ETH Zurich in Switzerland, where she is developing an analytical method that aims to revise the existing architectural history canon using cross-cultural perspectives using a case study from Japan.